NEW TAX
SECRETS

KEEP MORE OF *YOUR* RETIREMENT MONEY IN *YOUR* POCKET

Joseph S. Lucey, CFP®

Published by

BEVERLY HILLS PUBLISHING

468 Camden Drive

Beverly Hills, California 90210

Beverly Hills Publishing, LLC

www.beverlyhillspublishing.com

ISBN: 978-1-7378006-9-9

While the author has made every effort to provide accurate Internet addresses and other contact information at the time of publication, neither the publisher nor the author assumes any responsibility for errors, or for changes that occur after publication. Further, the publisher does not have any control over and does not assume any responsibility for author or third-party websites or their content.

The information provided herein is stated to be truthful and consistent. It is offered for informational purposes solely and is universal, as so. The presentation of the information is without contract or any type of guarantee assurance.

The trademarks that are used are without any consent, and the publication of the trademark is without permission or backing by the trademark owner. All trademarks and brands within this book are for clarifying purposes only and are owned by the owners themselves, not affiliated with this document.

Table of Contents

Acknowledgments

This book and my business would not have been possible without the help of my wife, Patty, the cofounder and vice president of Secured Retirement. Her encouragement in the development of my own company, her day-to-day involvement in the office, and her background in health-care matters are contributions I can't put a value on, and she prefers that I don't try. My work often involves doing educational seminars conducted at night, and Patty has always been there for our son in the times when I couldn't be. She takes pride in being "a hockey mom," and I will never be able to thank her enough for that.

A special thank you as well to my parents, Joe and Barb, who guided and encouraged me all along the way. My father, a 13-year officer in the Navy, taught me the kind of dedication and self-discipline that I've tried to bring to my family and my business.

I also wouldn't enjoy life as I do today without my son, Gavin, who indulges his father's love of hockey by allowing me to stay close to the sport through his own involvement.

On a professional level, Ed Slott—considered one of this country's foremost authorities on IRAs—has been a special mentor who has always been helpful in my career. I'm proud to be a member of his Ed Slott Master Elite IRA Advisors Group.

Thanks also to Advisors Excel, a group that has helped me expand and improve my business. Thanks also to the writers/editors who helped me prepare this book and another: Rick Dean, Lars Dolder and Allen Taylor, as well as Andrea Albright of Beverly Hills Publishing.

And a special thanks to my staff at Secured Retirement, present and past, as well as to all our friends and clients. Without you, there would be no point in writing a book.

And finally, a special shout-out to my beloved Minnesota Wild, the NHL team that helps keep my life interesting. And to the Minnesota Vikings, who of late have assured that I'll have Januarys and Februarys open without the worry of having to worry about their performance in the playoffs.

Introduction

Pliny the Elder had just bathed and eaten lunch when he sat down to relax at the imperial naval base at Misenum on August 24, 79 A.D. Misenum was situated on the northwest side of the Bay of Naples, Italy, overlooking the Mediterranean Sea. Pliny's nephew, the younger Pliny, a poet and scholar, was visiting from Rome.[1]

The weather had been fair in the few days since Pliny the Younger arrived, but there had been a few abnormalities. The family had felt several earth tremors, but, the younger Pliny later wrote in a letter, the earthquakes "were not particularly alarming because they [were] frequent in [the area]." In nearby cities, plumes of gas had been erupting from the ground. These had been misinterpreted by the superstitious people as giants perusing the cities' extremities. Whether giants or gaseous fumaroles, these peculiar events were ignored. By all accounts, it was a regular summer day in the Roman empire on August 24.

Then, a violent crack split the morning's silence. Pliny the Younger looked about frantically to identify the source. It didn't take long. In the distance, the peak of Mount Vesuvius had erupted in a billow of smoke and ash. The sky around its summit was darkening—the heavens swallowed by soot that eclipsed the sun. The elder Pliny jumped into action. He gathered his men and hastened across the bay, sailing for the port at Pompeii. He would never return.

Pliny the Younger and his mother were escorted aboard another ship heading in the opposite direction. As the two sailed for safety,

---

[1]Andrew Wallace-Hadrill. "Pompeii: Portents of Disaster." BBC.
https://www.bbc.co.uk/history/ancient/romans/pompeii_portents_01.shtml

they surely wondered what would befall the inhabitants of Pompeii and its surrounding towns.

For 24 hours, ash and pumice rained from above. Pompeii's inhabitants never stood a chance. Had they abandoned their homes immediately at the sight of Vesuvius's plumes of smoke, they may have cleared the lava's radius in time. However, most of the city folk underestimated the coming danger.

As ash fell in sheets, escape soon became impossible. Houses were shut in. The roads were rendered impassable. And the worst was yet to come.

At midnight, the first pyroclastic surges oozed from Vesuvius's crater. An avalanche of ash, rock, volcanic gas, and boiling lava rushed down the mountainside faster than a speeding chariot. The wall of fiery lava tore through the city, uninhibited by its piddly structures. The city's residents were instantly engulfed. They remained frozen in time for almost 2,000 years.

It's impossible to calculate exactly how many perished in the ancient city of Pompeii. But it's fair to assume that the casualties far exceeded the few thousand bodies that archaeologists have uncovered. Andrew Wallace-Hadrill, a professor of classics and the director of the British School at Rome, says, "The Romans were accustomed to losses mounting to tens of thousands in battle, and even they regarded this catastrophe as exceptional."

Perhaps the greatest tragedy in the epic story of Pompeii is that much of the loss of life might have been avoided. The people of Pompeii failed to recognize the signs of looming disaster, and it cost them their lives.

The Impending Eruption of the Tax Volcano

You've probably heard the saying, "Those who do not remember the past are condemned to repeat it." Philosopher George Santayana probably wasn't thinking of the destruction of Pompeii when he wrote that in his 1905 book, *The Life of Reason*. But as Santayana suggested, we should take a lesson from the condemned city lest we make the same mistake.

This is because there is an active volcano churning beneath our feet today, and one doesn't have to live near Mount St. Helens or Kilauea to be threatened by it. I'm talking here about the impending eruption of the "tax volcano," a force whose warning signs are as obvious—and too often ignored—as those of Vesuvius.

Let's take a minute to explain that.

The pool of molten rock that will eventually erupt to the surface is the tax-deferred money we've been acquiring and growing ever since we made our first contribution to an IRA, a 401(k), a 403(b), SEP, TSP (Thrift Savings Plan) or any other defined-contribution retirement plan. We made these contributions on a pretax basis, which seemed like a good deal when we were young workers with young families that needed every dollar we could get. Having tax-deferred contributions to our future removed from our tax obligation of the present was a gift horse whose teeth we never thought of examining.

There was a catch, of course, one we knew about and accepted with little question in our younger years.

The catch was that we would eventually pay tax on this growing pool of money at a later time in life. That time finally comes at age 72 when the IRS demands that we take fully taxable required distributions from our long-simmering tax-deferred accounts. These mandatory distributions—money we must take and pay tax on whether we need it for income or not—has the potential to (1) increase our marginal tax rate, (2) influence how much tax we pay on Social Security benefits, and (3) require that we pay more for Medicare premiums. These extra taxes can be especially hurtful in retirement, as every dollar spent on taxes is a dollar we can no longer pay ourselves at a time when regular paychecks stop coming.

Now, there is no way to completely shut off a smoldering volcano. But unlike the doomed citizens of Pompeii, there are things we can do to protect ourselves from the lethal lava, toxic fumes, and hot ash of the inevitable tax eruption. Which brings us to the purpose of this book.

We'll discuss later in these pages ways to reduce the bubbling pool of growing tax-deferred funds that will eventually burst to the surface. A major part of that discussion will involve reducing your tax burden now at a time when tax rates are at a historical low rather than paying these inevitable taxes at a time when rates are very likely to be higher.

We'll talk about using the tax-advantageous Roth IRA—through both contributions early in life and conversions later—as a means of reducing the pool. We'll also talk about ways to use charitable contributions—a big component of the TaxSmart Plan we will soon introduce—to reduce your tax obligation.

Before we get into all that, however, let's first look at the "sale on taxes" now available to Americans at the start of the 21st-century's third decade.

Why Now Is the Time to Address Your Taxes

A basic premise of tax planning says that if you are going to owe taxes on your retirement savings eventually, why not pay the bill at a time when taxes are as low as they've been in generations?

Such is the situation we encounter in 2022, the year this book was being completed. Simply put, there's never been a better time to address the U.S. income tax system. The 2017 Tax Cuts and Jobs Act—more commonly known as the "Trump tax cuts"—created a unique opportunity for lower taxes, one not seen since 1932.[2]

---

[2]Bradford Tax Institute. "History of Federal Income Tax Rates."
https://bradfordtaxinstitute.com/Free_Resources/Federal-Income-Tax-Rates.aspx

In that year, Congress raised taxes on the top earners from 25 percent to 63 percent. In 1944, the tax rate peaked at 94 percent for Americans earning more than $200,000.[3]

It was so bad then that Ronald Reagan, an actor before he became president, made just two movies a year and earned $100,000 per movie. His reason for not making more movies was that it didn't make financial sense when he kept just $6 for every $100 he earned.

As president from 1981, Reagan was successful in reducing the marginal tax rates Americans paid on their income. But even his cuts paled in comparison to those secured by President Donald Trump beginning in 2018. The following chart shows the difference in tax rates from 2017, before the implementation of the Tax Cuts and Jobs Act, to the levels of 2022.

Tax Rate Changes Over the Years

SINGLE FIILER				MARRIED FILING JOINTLY			
2017		2022		2017		2022	
10%	$0-$9,325	10%	$0-$10,275	10%	$0-$18,650	10%	$0-$20,550
15%	$9,326-$37,950	12%	$10,276-$41,775	15%	$18,651-$75,900	12%	$20,551-$83,550
25%	$37,951-$91,900	22%	$41,776-$89,075	25%	$75,901-$153,100	22%	$83,551-$178,150
28%	$91,901-$191,650	24%	$89,076-$170,050	28%	$153,101-$233,350	24%	$178,151-$340,100
33%	$191,651-$416,700	32%	$340,101-$431,900	33%	$233,351-$416,700	32%	$329,851-$418,850
35%	$416,701-$418,400	35%	$431,901-$647,850	35%	$416,701-$470,700	35%	$418,851-$628,300
39.6%	Over $418,400	37%	Over $647,851	39.6%	Over $470,701	37%	Over $628,300

Source: Taxfoundation.org

---

[3]Tax Foundation. "Federal Individual Income Tax Rates History." https://files.taxfoundation.org/legacy/docs/fed_individual_rate_history_nominal&adjusted-20110909.pdf

Yet the tax rates shown above are like a carton of milk; they have an expiration date. In this case, the Trump tax cuts are scheduled to "sunset" on December 31, 2025. Waiting until January 1, 2026, to start paying down the bill on your tax-deferred accounts is like drinking milk after its expiration date. Because we have no idea what tax rates will look like in 2026 or later, waiting until then to begin implementing tax strategies could be harmful to your fiscal health.

Beyond that, there is no guarantee that the Trump tax rates will survive through the end of 2025.

The COVID-19 pandemic changed much of the American economic outlook, as well as its debt picture. Believing that increased government spending was necessary to help many Americans survive the loss of jobs and wages during pandemic-related business shutdowns, the Trump administration spent $2.6 trillion on a stimulus package in 2020, and the administration of President Joe Biden another $1.9 trillion in March 2021. The national debt consequently rose to more than $28 *trillion*.[4]

What does this mean to our outlook on taxes? Well, in order to pay down national debt—if that is a goal—the U.S. must either (1) reduce spending or (2) increase taxes, or (3) do both. Given the historical tendency of Democrats to increase spending on social programs, it seems likely that Biden will eventually have to raise taxes to address our national debt. I wouldn't be surprised, in fact, if the Trump tax cuts were not eliminated even before their "sunset" date.

And so the question becomes: When faced with a "pay me now or pay me later" proposition on the tax-deferred money you've saved over a lifetime of hard work, would you rather pay your inevitable tax on this money at a 12 percent rate now or a 15 percent rate (if not

---

[4]Rob Berger. "5 Breathtaking Numbers Reveal The Unsettling Cost Of Stimulus." Forbes. https://www.forbes.com/sites/robertberger/ 2020/10/18/5-big-numbers-reveal-the-unsettling-scope-of-stimulus-spending/?sh=1ffb6704142b

higher) later? At 22 percent now or 25 percent a few years from now? At 24 percent now or 28 percent after 2025 (if not sooner)?

Given the assumption that tax rates will go up, the only question is, how soon? And, how much?

Don't Wait to Begin Proactive Tax Planning

When most people think about retirement planning, they think about working with a financial adviser and other finance professionals to accumulate wealth and plan their investment strategies. While wealth accumulation and strategic investment planning are important as retirement planning best practices, just as important are distribution strategies that involve income planning and how to take that income in the most tax-advantageous way possible. The challenge in doing this can be addressed in the following three questions:

- How do I take back this tax-deferred money I've been saving?
- How do I make this income tax efficient?
- How do I make this income last a lifetime?

Focusing on tax strategies, such as those we'll describe in this book, is definitely the first step toward making sure that your retirement journey is as successful as it can be.

The last thing anyone should want is to end up on someone else's retirement plan. When it comes to taxation throughout retirement years, every situation is different. That means you should have your own custom plan—a plan with a purpose. You want to be proactive, not reactive.

Government-imposed plans often force retirees to keep their retirement assets in a specific account for a long duration of time. The rules prohibit access to some or all of the money in your IRA, 401(k), or 403(b) account until you are 59½ years old. But at age 72, retirees are forced to begin withdrawing money and paying the taxes owed on those withdrawals.

The magic age for Required Minimum Distributions (RMDs) was 70½ from 1986 until December 2019 when it was changed to age 72. Today, anyone born after July 1, 1949, is subject to the age requirement change.[5] If you are wealthy and have a large retirement account, this change will affect you more than anyone else.

IRAs and other tax-deferred retirement plans are the only assets that people are told they have to liquidate at some point in their lifetime. What people are not told, however, is the future tax rate they will have to pay when they begin this mandatory liquidation. If the tax rate is higher during your retirement years, then you keep less of your money when you need it most.

This is a reactive plan. A more proactive approach, however, uses today's all-time low rates to your advantage. You start to reposition your assets today while tax rates are known (and known to be lower) so that you can avoid the uncertainty of the future. You have no idea what the tax obligation on your own withdrawal strategy will look like 10 or 20 years down the road. Your best-case scenario is to reduce your future (and unknown) tax obligation now at a time when tax rates are known to be at their lowest point in years.

Reducing Taxes Is Your Right

The number one fallacy told to Boomers throughout their lifetimes is that they'd be putting money into their tax-deferred retirement accounts while in a higher tax bracket, then withdrawing that money at a lower tax bracket when their income (and income taxes) is lower during retirement. Thousands of retirees are waking up to reality, however, and finding that is not the case. They may actually end up paying more in taxes in retirement than they were when putting money into those tax-deferred accounts.

---

[5]"Retirement Topics: Required Minimum Distributions." May 3, 2021. https://www.irs.gov/retirement-plans/plan-participant-employee/ retirement-topics-required-minimum-distributions-rmds

Think about that for a minute.

One way of reducing taxes is to reduce income, but that's hardly an effective strategy. I mean, does the retirement of your dreams include tightening your belt just to keep your tax bill low? That's not how most people view their "golden years." In fact, most people today find they need a retirement income that is roughly equal to, or possibly even higher than, what they knew during their years in the daily workforce.

The challenge in retirement tax planning, then, is to find legal ways to keep one's marginal tax rates as low as possible. A plan that effectively does this allows you to keep more of your hard-earned money, which should be a basic retirement goal.

Keep in mind, too, that reducing one's tax obligation is a concept 180 degrees removed from what most people call "tax cheating" or "tax fraud." One of the most prominent legal scholars in American history, U.S. federal judge Learned Hand (1909–1951), famously opined that citizens have no patriotic duty to increase their taxes. In fact, he went on to say, "There is nothing sinister in so arranging affairs as to keep taxes as low as possible."

Supreme Court Justice Louis Brandeis, who sat on the high court from 1916 to 1939, compared tax avoidance with his personal experience in using a toll bridge. He said:

I live in Alexandria, Virginia. Near the Supreme Court chambers is a toll bridge across the Potomac. When in a rush, I pay the dollar toll and get home early. However, I usually drive outside the downtown section of the city and cross the Potomac on a free bridge. This bridge was placed outside the downtown Washington, DC area to serve a useful social service, getting drivers to drive the extra mile and help alleviate congestion during the rush hour. If I went over the toll bridge and through the barrier without paying the toll, I would be committing tax evasion ... If, however, I drive the extra mile and drive outside the city of Washington to the free bridge, I am using a legitimate, logical and suitable method of tax avoidance, and am performing a useful social service by doing so. For my tax evasion, I should be punished. For my tax avoidance, I should be commended. The tragedy of life today is that so few people know that the free bridge even exists.

I'm of the same opinion as Hand and Brandeis. A good citizen may actually want to do everything within their power to avoid and reduce taxes. The purpose of this book is to help you do that.

How I Fell in Love with Tax Planning

Since the age of seven, I've gravitatEd toward financial planning. I'd wake up, turn on PBS, and watch a show called *Wall Street Week* with Louis Rukeyser. Most adults found it boring, but I found the discussions fascinating.

At 13, my school had a "follow an adult to work" day and I went to work with a neighbor who was a stockbroker. This was before widespread computer usage. When I walked into his office and saw all the ticker tape and quotes on computer screens, I thought that was pretty neat.

I left home shortly after high school graduation and joined the Marine Corps. After six years, I went back home and worked as a bartender while attending the University of Minnesota. Every day at 3:15 p.m., a group of stockbrokers came into the bar for happy hour. It was fascinating to listen in on their conversations and hear the stories they'd tell. After a while, one of them hired me to make cold calls and that led to me opening some accounts on his behalf. A branch manager saw that I had promise and offered me a job as a financial advisor.

In 1994, I earned my financial planning license.

Today, my Midwest-based Secured Retirement firm works with a lot of clients throughout the nation with our TaxSmart™ retirement program. The vast majority of them are between 55 and 70 years of age. As such, most have needs that are very different from those they knew as younger workers and investors. We work hard to understand

and address those different needs as our clients approach a new and unique period of life.

A Different Approach to Financial Planning

I'm really passionate about the difference between my financial planning firm's approach and the wealth accumulation and investment strategies most financial advisers spend their time on. To be sure, wealth accumulation and investment strategies are part of what we do. But the biggest difference in our approach, I believe, is in the way we incorporate tax and income planning into a financial/retirement plan.

As fiduciaries, we're obligated to put the best interests of our clients first. Consequently, we believe one of our highest priorities is to help them reduce their taxes, one of the largest expenses they will encounter as they transition into retirement.

Most clients we work with don't consider themselves wealthy. They consider themselves middle class. High net worth individuals hire financial advisers to morally, ethically, and legally reduce their taxes over time. They use the secrets I will share in this book, and I believe it's time everyone else gets a chance to take advantage of the same strategies.

But not everyone in my industry shares my view on the importance of developing tax strategies. Let's look at some reasons why.

First, most advisers do not get paid based on the amount of planning they do. They're paid more typically on the size of the assets and investments they manage, or they get commissions from insurance products and investment transactions.

The second theme is it's difficult to get paid for tax-saving strategies. Most consumers have a hard time justifying the value. If your financial advisor saves you thousands of dollars in taxes, what is a fair value for that?

The consumer wants tax savings, but they don't want to pay their adviser for the benefit. Still, the financial adviser wants to be compensated for providing that benefit. It's almost a conflict of interest.

Because of that conflict, financial advisers end up focusing on strategies that pay them the most. That includes investment strategies, transactions, and allocation.

Even the largest institutions—mutual fund companies, Wall Street brokerage firms, and so on—are hesitant to provide tax-saving advice to their clients. Large brokerage firms, what I call "big box brokerage firms," face compliance issues in offering financial advice based on future tax rates that are unknown. Unless they are a CPA, they will have a difficult time. They don't get paid to give tax advice, even if they provide discount, no-cost, or low-cost mutual fund accounts.

Due to these challenges, most people don't get solid tax-saving advice for retirement. That's why I wrote this book. My goal is to make sure you get the advice you need to retire well with minimal taxation.

CHAPTER 1

Kill the Tax Beast

October 7, 2007, was one of the best and most stressful days of my life. It was the day my son, Gavin, was born, and we weren't sure he'd survive. Born premature, he weighed only three pounds and fifteen ounces.

The first few days were harrowing. But the doctors and hospital staff who attended to our boy were outstanding. We're forever grateful to them for their diligence and professionalism.

From the day he was born, Gavin and my wife were tied at the hip. Not a single day passed in the first two years of his life that they didn't spend together. Shortly after Gavin turned two, my wife went away for a weekend. It would be my first time being the solo parent for the entire weekend. I was ecstatic. Finally, it was my time to shine, but I was a little nervous to take on the responsibility alone!

Things got off to a good start. Gavin and I went to the park and played on the slides. I pushed him around on his little tricycle. We ate ice cream. We built blocks. Gavin kicked over the blocks and we rebuilt them again. The entire day was dedicated to his favorite things. But something seemed a little askew. All day, Gavin seemed a little out of sorts. Eventually, I figured out why—he missed his mother.

I don't know why it didn't occur to me earlier that it might be upsetting for my two-year-old son to be away from his mother. But as the day progressed, it became abundantly clear—Gavin wanted Mom. And I wasn't sure that Dad alone was going to cut it.

As his cries intensified, I knew I couldn't call my wife. That'd be admitting failure, right? And if she came home early, it would end the daddy-son weekend I had planned. So, I called my next best resource—my mother.

Mom had raised three children. I figured she'd know what to do. She must have anticipated I'd have some difficulty because I could almost hear the smirk on her face when she asked, "How's it going?"

I filled her in on my predicament and she laughed.

"First of all," she said, "stop giving him so many activities. He's tired. He'll get crankier the more tired he gets. And cut out all the sweets."

She instructed me to give him a bottle (½ apple juice, ½ water just as he preferred) and put on one of his favorite movies.

I looked around frantically for a children's DVD movie and settled for the Disney classic *Beauty and the Beast*.

If you've seen *Beauty and the Beast*, you know how the story goes. There's a beautiful girl named Belle (which means "beauty" in French). She dreams of a fairytale life, but then everything goes wrong. Belle's father is captured by a terrible beast that lives beyond the village. The beautiful, unselfish person that she is, Belle convinces the beast to imprison her in her father's stead.

It's sometime around this point in the story that the villagers convene to form an angry mob. It's a pivotal scene in the movie's development. They gather their pitchforks and torches, planning on the tactics necessary to rid the peaceful village of the monster that is among them. And during this dark scene the villagers resolve to do one thing … *kill the beast*!

You are likewise confronted with a beast. A tax beast.

Of course, in Disney's rendition of *Beauty and the Beast*, the beast is tragically misunderstood. He's actually gentle and kind. A gentle prince is trapped within a furry exterior.

In real life, things don't work out so nicely. There is no fairytale ending to the dilemma that 21st-century retirees are facing. The tax beast is not a misunderstood prince. It is every bit a snarling, rabid monster that will tear apart your hard-earned investment portfolio and upend your retirement plans if you're not prepared.

It's time to kill the tax beast.

What the Financial Media Doesn't Tell You

Few people understand the importance of tax planning in the long-term viability of a retirement plan. That's unfortunate, as the tax strategies I'll share in this book can be a primary determiner in whether a family can retire well and in what tax bracket.

Why don't more people know, or take the time to learn, about tax-planning techniques that can save them tens of thousands, if not hundreds of thousands in taxes over the course of a lifetime?

One reason is that their financial advisers emphasize investment and wealth accumulation strategies, but they don't emphasize nearly enough tax planning and income planning strategies.

There are other reasons as well.

The advent of the 401(k), 403(b), IRA, and other tax-deferred retirement accounts has confused the issue for many people. The IRA was created in 1974 with the passage of the Employee Retirement Income Security Act (ERISA). In order to open one, an individual had to have a custodian. That was usually a bank or brokerage firm that specialized in selling stocks, bonds, and other financial assets. Dispensing tax advice was never part of the job description.

In 1978, Congress passed legislation that allowed employees to defer taxes on deferred compensation. It didn't take long for companies to begin offering this benefit to employees, allowing them to sock money away into a tax-deferred savings account for retirement purposes.

The 403(b) precedes both IRA and 401(k) accounts. Created in 1958, its purpose is to provide a tax-sheltered annuity for employees of public organizations and 501(c)(3) organizations.

All of these tax-deferred retirement plans have one thing in common—they allowed what I call the "Grand Illusion" to develop.

The Grand Illusion is this: If you put money into your IRA, 401(k), or 403(b) plan to save for retirement, you will pay less in taxes when you access the money during your retirement because your income will be lower. This misconception is based on a couple of assumptions:

1) The first assumption is that the tax rate when you put your money into your retirement account will be higher than the tax rate when you take it out. We've been told this now for several generations. Someone sat us down and said, "Kid, take a tax deduction on your salary now, set the money aside and let compounding interest do its thing. Then when you have less income in retirement, you'll pay less in taxes on this money when you finally need it." For many years, that prospect might have been true. But tax rates change depending on congressional legislation and interpretation of that legislation by the executive branch, which means that tax rates could potentially change from one election cycle to another.

2) The second assumption is that everyone's income needs will be lower after retirement. In fact, that's not the case. There are many factors that determine a family's income needs. In some cases, retiree income needs increase after retirement. In fact, it is becoming more evident that as America recovers from the COVID pandemic, we may begin experiencing the kind of inflation many Boomers only recall from the late 1970s. In December of 2022, in fact, year-over-year inflation reached 7 percent—an increase not seen since 1982.[6] A post-pandemic

---

[6]"Inflation rises 7% over the past year, highest since 1982." Jan. 12, 2022. www.cnbc.com

demand for additional goods and services that were no longer readily available because of labor shortages and supply-chain breakdowns created higher costs for food, groceries, fuel and health care. Such increases seem certain to require even greater levels of income to maintain a retiree's standard of living, which could mean greater withdrawals from tax-deferred retirement accounts. And that, of course, means higher taxes.

Then there are the things we weren't told.

Because the retirement planning industry is focused primarily on wealth accumulation, many financial planners concentrate more on selling products instead of analyzing each family's future income and tax planning needs. As a result, many consumers have been shortchanged. The priority of investing for wealth accumulation alone while downplaying future tax and income concerns has led the average saver to getting incomplete or bad advice. As a result, many consumers found themselves owning financial products that do nothing to address future tax concerns, but are of considerable benefit to the financial professionals and firms that sold them.

On another note, the financial media fails to tell the full story when it focuses on information that is easy to convey to the consumer. That typically is information related to wealth accumulation, portfolio growth, and expense reduction related to that portfolio. Getting the average consumer to understand, or even think about, the future tax implications of such a portfolio is something few media sources care to deal with.

These information sources rarely bother to explain, for instance, how a $1 million balance in a Roth IRA—an account funded with after-tax dollars—is actually worth more than a traditional IRA with the same account value.

The traditional IRA, remember, has been funded by pretax money and has grown on a tax-deferred basis over time. But taxes on that money must be paid eventually, meaning its true value is considerably less than the $1 million shown on the bottom line of a quarterly account statement. Money in the Roth IRA, however, grows and can be withdrawn on a tax-free basis. What you see on your account statement is what you get. That important distinction, in my opinion, is one that receives far too little attention in the information presented to the average retirement account investor.

Consider, too, the level of guidance—or lack thereof—provided to investors in a company-sponsored retirement savings plan such as a 401(k).

As noted previously, such plans must have a professional custodian, often a financial management company, but the custodian's duties generally deal more with accounting than advising. A custodian might offer some general guidance on asset allocation—an age-appropriate blend of stocks and bonds, for instance. But these observations are generally based on modern portfolio theory and not on what is best for an individual investor or family. Moreover, the average 401(k) participant is generally limited in investment choices to the financial products—typically mutual funds—offered within a company's plan.

As a result, guidance on the future tax implications of tax-deferred retirement plans is largely unavailable to the typical 401(k) participant. Many families consequently will face a future tax bill that is a significant drain on their retirement savings. This is a tax bill, mind you, that could be greatly reduced with effective tax planning.

Finding such planning, however, is sometimes easier said than done.

People seek professional financial help for a variety of reasons. Many are interested in building a long-range retirement plan, one that provides a lifelong income stream. Others seek advice on paying off their mortgage early, reducing taxes, planning for long-term health care, finding affordable health insurance, and selecting Social Security benefits.

But not all financial professionals are eager to provide that kind of help. They instead guide clients toward mutual funds and/or other investment products promoted by their parent companies or are part of their favorite investment strategies. Providing tax advice, however, often isn't a part of their agenda.

Beyond that, some advisors don't deal with tax matters because they are not paid to do so. Many advisors are paid based on "assets under management," which puts a premium on selling and growing value in the financial products they offer. Time spent on planning and dispensing advice isn't compensated the way it is for, say, an attorney who charges by the hour—even if they only spend 10 minutes of that hour dealing with your specific issue. (Nice work if you can get it.)

We approach things differently at Secured Retirement, my company based in St. Louis Park, Minnesota, a first-tier Twin Cities suburb. We believe that providing advice on tax and income planning is as essential to our clients—if not more so—than the investment counseling we routinely provide, and we are happy to do so.

Don't Ignore the Hurricane Warnings

Another big flaw of the financial industry is that, so many times, financial decisions are based on reactions to specific events. Investors aren't proactive but reactive.

Let me try to illustrate what I mean.

During my service in the U.S. Marine Corps, I spent much of my time stationed in Beaufort, South Carolina. Being a coastal community, we always knew when a hurricane was forecast. When we heard a hurricane was coming, people would rush to grocery stores and clear the shelves of emergency supplies, then put up shutters and board up their homes for protection. Sometimes, the storm hit head-on and did a lot of damage. Other times, there was merely minor damage. But we always knew when the hurricane was coming and could be proactive in protecting ourselves.

By contrast, you quite often don't know when a tornado is coming until it appears out of nowhere.

I've also spent much of my life in the Midwest, specifically Minnesota where tornadoes are prevalent. Maybe not as prevalent as Kansas, Oklahoma, or Texas, but still a weather concern you become accustomed to watching for. When you hear the siren notifying you there's a tornado in your vicinity, it's too late to prepare. You can't board up the home or run to the grocery store for more water. You head for the nearest shelter and hope for the best.

When planning for retirement, the proactive approach requires thinking in advance of the storm. Specifically, it requires thinking about how taxes might increase during retirement, and then planning for that likelihood. It's more like planning for a hurricane than a tornado. You know you'll have to pay taxes on your income even if you don't know exactly what the tax rate will be when you retire. Still, you can be proactive and prepare for the worst-case scenario.

Too many families, however, fail to heed the warning signs. They fail to see the huge tax storm coming and end up reacting to a financial crisis.

The proactive approach to retirement planning recognizes that a tax hurricane is looming. It is time to board up windows, store the lawn furniture, and stock up on food staples and water. A reactive approach ignores the pending storm and wonders why we were hit with a tornado suddenly, with no time to prepare.

Tax Secret #1	Don't be reactive; be proactive with your retirement planning.

A Historical Look at Tax Rates; How National Debt Affects Our Future

Earlier, I mentioned Ronald Reagan and how, because of high tax rates, he made just two movies a year during part of his acting career.

If he could only keep $6 for every $100 he earned, he'd effectively made only $6,000 per movie after the second one.

Tax rates have come down a lot since then. In 1981, when Reagan took office, the top tax rate was 70 percent. One year later, it was 50 percent.[7] Since then, tax rates have come down even further.

In 2017, a married couple filing jointly with taxable income (gross income minus a standard tax deduction) of $250,000 would have been taxed at 33 percent.[8] Today, they'd be taxed at 24 percent. Families have a unique opportunity right now to move massive amounts of money at less cost than just three years ago. The standard deduction is higher and the tax rate is the lowest it's been in 40 years.

How long these low rates remain in effect, however, is anybody's guess.

Typically, when Congress proposes tax cuts or makes changes to the tax code, there's a negotiation process. There is a lot of back-and-forth between Republicans and Democrats on the House floor, in addition to "backroom" agreements between individual members of Congress where they promise to vote on each other's proposed legislation and support certain causes. President Trump was able to pass his tax cuts without a lot of that negotiating because, even with 12 House Republicans voting against the legislation, it still passed 227 to 203 with no Democratic votes. The outcome was much thinner in the Senate, but it passed.

While the Republicans had the numbers to pass the bill, a "sunset" provision needed to be added to the legislation due to budget rules that prevent deficit spending. That's why a sunset date was set for December 31, 2025.

Tax laws are written with these considerations in mind. But it's important to note that the Tax Cut and Jobs Act of 2017 was passed at

---

[7]Tax Brackets. https://www.tax-brackets.org/ federaltaxtable/1977

[8]2020 Federal Tax Rates. https://www.irs.com/articles/
2020-federal-tax-rates-brackets-standard-deductions/

a different time with different economic conditions. The economy was doing well, and it was doing even better after the tax cuts.

Then, COVID-19 hit, unexpectedly, like a tornado. That changed everything.

The year 2020 will go down in history as a major economic event. The loss of lives was devastating enough. But so too was the loss of jobs and income—to say nothing of lost tax revenue—due to the pandemic-related closing of businesses both big and small. Never before has so much national debt been accumulated in such a short time. While Trump was planning to expand his tax cuts, the pandemic changed everyone's priorities.

The tax cuts themselves expanded the U.S. debt profile. When you add in the $4.4 trillion stimulus packages that sought to help people deal with the financial losses from the pandemic, our national debt grew to nearly $28 trillion.[9] It's continuing to grow even as you read this. As interest rates go up, the maintenance on that debt will explode and the amount of money needed to pay it off will go through the roof.

Democrats and Republicans frequently argue over the best way to pay down the national debt. One idea is to cut spending, but not everyone agrees. The Keynesian theory of economics believes that government spending is the best way to keep the economy growing, while the "trickle-down" approach argues that the best way to prompt economic growth is by reducing spending and taxes to put more money into the economy, money that eventually will be taxed on a transactional basis. We're divided. About half the country favors more government services while the other half favors tax cuts and expense reduction.

The difference between the Keynesian view and the trickle-down view, popularized by Reagan when he was president, is huge. It's one of the reasons the nation is so polarized. But political sentiments and

---

[9]Therese M. Cruciano and Michael Strudler. "Individual Income Tax Rates and Tax Shares, 1993." https://www.irs.gov/pub/irs-soi/93inintrts.pdf

movements go in cycles. That's why I'm sure that we're in for a big change sometime in the next decade.

We've had a good run with low tax rates for a while now, but I have concerns that the good times may end soon. Reagan ushered in a golden era where trickle-down economics gained favor among a good crosscurrent of the electorate. However, it won't be long before the political environment shifts again toward the Keynesians. When that happens, the only way families will be able to isolate themselves from increased taxes is to focus on tax-reduction strategies.

Our exploding national debt will play the biggest role in the ever-changing political picture that will soon, I predict, lead to higher tax rates.

The current debt situation for the U.S. is unprecedented. Never before have we seen the national debt rise as high as it did in 2020 and '21. After World War II, for example, the percentage of debt to gross domestic product (GDP) was understandably high, 113 percent in 1946.[10] Well, it's 102 percent today after we added over $3 trillion of debt in one year to fight the economic effects of the pandemic. Let's also consider this: the total cost of World War II in today's dollars was $4.1 trillion, about $1 trillion more than what the Trump administration piled on in a single year.[11]

Immediately after World War II, the government set out to pay down the war-related debt. It was largely successful in doing so. By 1974, our debt-to-GDP ratio fell to 24 percent.[12]

---

[10]"War Debt: America's Cost of Going to War." https://www.debt.org/blog/war-debt-america/

[11]"National Debt." History.com. https://www.history.com/topics/us-government/national-debt

[12]"The Long Story of U.S. Debt." The Atlantic. https://www.theatlantic.com/business/archive/2012/11/the-long-story-of-us-debt-from-1790-to-2011-in-1-little-chart/265185/

Yet, in the year 2021, the U.S. is once again expected to have a ballooning national debt that exceeds our GDP. And now the question you should be asking is whether America is prepared to make the same sacrifices to get out of this conundrum that we took to build our way out of debt following World War II. Are we prepared to make the hard decision to cut spending, or will we try to tax our way out of the debt crater?

My personal opinion: I think we're in for a long haul of increased taxation.

While we have a high debt-to-GDP ratio right now, the fortunate thing is our interest rates are low. You don't have to go any further than your local bank to see that. Still, we have not reduced spending on entitlements and other government-sponsored benefits. We spend a great deal on social programs such as Medicare, health care, and education. That makes our national debt scarier because half the country wants to expand these programs.

Bottom line, what all of this means is that the future is uncertain. We don't know what the tax rate on families will be 10 or 20 years from now. If history is a guide, the U.S. is headed for a discussion on how to pay down the national debt. As soon as the fight against COVID-19 is won, I would expect the attention of elected representatives to turn toward paying off this debt. They will have to either focus on cutting spending or raising taxes, or both. My best guess is that raising taxes will definitely occur sooner rather than later. If not when the Trump tax cuts reach their sunset deadline in December 2025, then sooner. The opportunity for you to address proactive tax planning is now. Time is ticking away.

Tax Secret #2	It is a myth that tax rates in retirement will be lower than your earning years. Tax rates will likely increase from 40-year lows in the very near future. Learn how investments will be taxed in retirement and plan accordingly to reduce taxable income on tax returns.

It is time, right now, to plan for the eventuality that taxes are most certainly about to increase substantially and could be a potential problem with your retirement security.

We're looking at a hurricane.

CHAPTER 2

Seeing Through the Grand Illusion*

(* With thanks to Styx for one of my all-time favorite rock songs)

Meet Ronnie and Melissa Olson, a fictional couple in a real-life situation.

Ronnie and Melissa have three children. Ronnie, a good husband and father, was in the military until his youngest child turned 13. When he left the service at age 32, he had 12 honorable years behind him. The family sold their home in Texas, where Ronnie had been stationed, and moved back to Minnesota where the couple dated as high school sweethearts and where most of the family still resided. They hope to live there for the rest of their lives.

Ronnie, making use of the leadership skills he picked up in the armed forces, landed a job with 3M at its Maplewood facility in the Twin Cities area. Over time he worked his way up into a mid-level management position in the company. Melissa, once their kids became more active in junior high and high school and less dependent on a stay-at-home mother, resumed her teaching career, initially as a substitute before moving to full-time status.

In the service, Ronnie was an enlisted guy, which didn't always provide a lot of disposable income for his young family. Much of their military years were spent living paycheck to paycheck leaving little for investments for their future retirement. Ronnie made enough to support his family, but they didn't have a large savings account when transitioning from the military back into the civilian lifestyle.

Ronnie was well into his second career before he could really start saving and planning for retirement. He began to make consistent tax-deferred contributions—what the IRS calls "qualified contributions"—to his 401(k) plan. Melissa eventually did the same to a 403(b)-plan available to her as a public employee. But with three kids to feed, they could hardly max out their contributions from year to year. In other words, the Olsons are a typical American family, saving what they could whenever they could afford to do so.

But as time passed and promotions increased his income, Ronnie began to increase his qualified retirement contributions into the 401(k) plan at 3M.

At the age of 50, after helping their youngest daughter with a reasonable wedding and her now starting her own family, he began maximizing his annual contributions. He also began making annual "catch-up" contributions allowed for people over age 50. He was just a few years from retirement when his mother passed and Ronnie inherited farm property that was producing regular rental income, money he and Melissa decided to earmark for retirement. Slowly and surely, they began making up for the years when they were unable to save as much as they might have liked.

Ronnie retired in 2017 at age 68 after a 36-year career at 3M. He left with a nice pension from the company and a monthly Social Security payment that was enhanced by some 16 percent because he waited two full years after his full retirement age (66) to begin taking benefits.

For four years he and Melissa (who retired from teaching two years earlier) lived the retirement of their dreams. They spent more time with friends and grandkids, did some traveling, became more serious about their hobbies. The couple was justifiably proud of what they had saved for their future. They owned their home and their retirement account balances had a combined net worth of more than $1 million—something the younger Ronnie Olson, who lived paycheck to paycheck for so many years, never would have thought possible.

But in 2021 Ronnie turned 72 and suddenly the Olsons were looking at a tax situation they also had never imagined.

This was the year Ronnie had to begin taking fully taxable Required Minimum Distributions (RMDs) from his 401(k) that had grown through the workings of compound interest and better-than-normal market growth to a value of some $650,000.

Ronnie's first RMD was $25,400, a figure determined by dividing the total of his tax-deferred money ($650,000) by a "life expectancy factor" determined by the IRS (25.6 at age 72).[13] The couple didn't need or especially want the money they are required to withdraw; they would have preferred to continue growing it. But take it they must, and in doing so they incur additional taxes on the amount withdrawn. They are shocked to find that they are now paying taxes at a higher rate than when they first made contributions to their retirement accounts in their 30s and 40s—the exact opposite of what they were told to expect.

And their concerns don't end there.

The Olsons were living comfortably in retirement on around $152,000 in gross income. They received Social Security benefits totaling almost $58,000, pension payments totaling around $70,000 from 3M and the Minnesota public employees' pension fund, and another $24,000 in rental income from the farmland.

Now suddenly they must add another $25,400 in unwanted taxable income to their total. Their modified adjusted gross income (MAGI) now exceeds $176,000, the 2021 threshold above which a couple

---

[13]The IRS changed its Uniform Life expectancy tables in 2022. By raising the life expectancy factors to reflect longer longevity, the service raised the divisor in the RMD calculation and consequently lowered the amount of distribution required. Had Ronnie taken his first RMD on his $650,000 401(k) in 2022, his amount would have been $23,722 ($650,000/27.4). Source: "IRS publishes new RMD tables." Dec. 8, 2021. www.advisors.principal.com

filing jointly must pay a surcharge on their monthly Medicare Part B premiums. Most Americans in 2021 paid a monthly Part B premium of $148.50, but people exceeding the MAGI threshold paid $207.90—an annual increase of $1,415 for a couple.

The outlook for 2022 is even more expensive. Couples whose MAGI exceeds $182,000 will pay monthly Part B premiums of $238 each.[14] That's an additional $1,632 for such a couple, $217 more than the previous year.

(For the record, an estimated 93 percent of Americans who are not subject to Medicare surcharges also will pay more in 2022 as the basic monthly premium saw an inflation-induced increase to $170, the largest single-year increase in Medicare history.)

The tax volcano, just like Mount Vesuvius, has just erupted on the Olsons.

They are being forced to take money out of their retirement account and pay taxes on it at a higher rate than expected, and at an age when they need to keep as much of their money as they can. Then there are "hidden taxes" such as the Medicare premiums that kick in. Our couple is now likely wondering why they hadn't known about these new retirement-time taxes earlier, and perhaps done something earlier to head them off.

Who is IRMAA, and Why Is She Hiking My Taxes?

You can hardly blame the Olsons for never having heard of IRMAA, a part of a 2003 law designed to overhaul the Medicare system. Most Americans also aren't familiar with it.

The income-related monthly adjustment amount is an effort to means-test the cost of Medicare. Translated, our government believes that people with significant "means"—that is, wealth—should pay

---

[14]"2022 Medicare Parts A and B Premiums." Centers for Medicare and Medicaid Services. www.cms.gov

more for government-provided health care for seniors, as illustrated in the below chart.

Part B Medicare Premium Variations

2022 PART B COSTS

If your yearly income in 2020 (for what you pay in 2022) was			You pay each month (in 2022)
File individual tax return	File joint tax return	File married & separate tax return	
$91,000 or less	$182,000 or less	$91,000 or less	$170.10
above $91,000 up to $114,000	above $182,000 up to $228,000	Not applicable	$238.10
above $114,000 up to $142,000	above $228,000 up to $284,000	Not applicable	$340.20
above $142,000 up to $170,000	above $284,000 up to $340,000	Not applicable	$442.30
above $170,000 and less than $500,000	above $340,000 and less than $750,000	above $91,000 and less than $409,000	$544.30
$500,000 or above	$750,000 and above	$409,000 and above	$578.30

Source: "Part B costs," www.medicare.gov

IRMAA, it could be argued, is a health insurance premium, not taxation. But the calculation is derived purely from your 1040 tax statement. In my definition of taxation, higher Medicare premiums calculated off a tax return alone can be called nothing other than an additional tax. It's just one example of what I consider a hidden tax, one that penalizes people who grew wealth more effectively than their neighbors.

And it isn't the only retirement tax to sneak up on many Americans.

The Olsons didn't know until just shortly before filing for Social Security that their monthly benefits were taxable. Indeed, Social Security recipients with provisional incomes of more than $32,000 (for married couples filing jointly) will pay tax at their ordinary rate on up to 50 percent of their benefits. The percentage of benefits subject to taxation rises to 85 percent for couples with provisional incomes exceeding $44,000, a figure that can hardly be considered "wealthy" by today's standards.

(We'll discuss provisional income and look at Social Security in more detail in the upcoming chapter.)

But then, why would the Olsons know all the consequences of their tax-deferred retirement plans? They only did what most Americans were advised to do throughout their working years. They saved for their future by putting a little of each paycheck into tax-deferred retirement accounts. Doing so on a pretax basis provided an immediate tax break and extra income that was especially important for workers with young families. This "qualified" money then had the opportunity to grow through years of compounded growth in whatever investment vehicles a company plan allowed. It seemed like a win-win scenario, even when considering the "strings attached" at the end of the deal.

The Olsons understood (as most Americans do) that they would eventually pay tax on all this qualified money upon withdrawing it. It was part of the deal we all made when putting our first dollar into an IRA, 401(k), 403(b), 457 plan, or other deferred contribution plans. They also eventually learned about an age, now 72, at which they would be required to start withdrawing money and paying taxes on the amounts taken. Again, all part of the deal.

What they hadn't realized, however, was the effect these withdrawals could have on their overall tax structure in retirement. They were, quite simply, taken in by the Grand Illusion, the idea that they would be paying less tax in retirement.

The taxes many people incur then are what I call "phantom taxes." Let's explain that.

Let's say I experience a routine financial transaction—a dividend from a stock or mutual fund, a capital gain from the growth or sale of an asset, a distribution from a retirement account—that produces a taxable event. This additional taxable income can do more than just add to my overall tax bill; it also can generate additional taxes you never saw coming. Your Social Security benefits, for example, might be taxed at a higher level. Your Medicare premiums also could increase. You could be elevated into a higher tax bracket.

These "phantom taxes," in short, are some we may not know much about during our time in the daily workforce, but discover very suddenly—and sometimes painfully—in retirement.

The Worst Investment Advice of the Past 40 Years

I sometimes wonder what the world was thinking in the many years when people believed things we now know aren't even close to being true.

I can imagine, for example, a father in Spain in, say, 1491 standing with his son on a cliff overlooking the Atlantic Ocean. "What's out there beyond what we can see?" the young boy asks. "Nothing," his papa replies. "Our world is flat. You sail to the end and you fall off the edge."

A year later, Christopher Columbus challenged that belief by sailing without falling off the edge and discovering what he called "a new world," never mind that it was already inhabited. A few years later in 1519, Ferdinand Magellan kept on sailing until he returned to the place from where he began, effectively ending the flat-earth theory.

There also was a time when learned physicians believed that bloodletting was the way to cure a serious illness. Legend has it that physicians attending to George Washington drained an estimated 40 percent of his blood in attempting to relieve what our first president initially believed was a cold. The patient didn't survive the cure.

I guess we shouldn't laugh at things people once just assumed to be true. Not when we have some of our own misperceptions even today.

I keep coming back to the flawed thinking that led financial professionals—in addition to well-meaning family members and friends—to advise younger workers that the money they put away in tax-deferred retirement accounts would be taxed at a lower rate when they withdraw this money in retirement. In the words of an old Broadway song, it ain't necessarily so.

If it sounds like I'm spreading a conspiracy theory, that somehow all the financial wizards got together and tried to pull the wool over your eyes, let me assure you that's not what I'm saying. No one lied to you on purpose or was trying to hurt you. But they were operating on some bad assumptions, just as the flat-earthers of Columbus's time did.

I believe economists, financial advisors, and your employers were just assuming that tax rates would be lower when you retire and have a reduction in income. This may well be the case for some Americans. For many others, however, this isn't their reality.

Many seniors in today's world, in fact, have a goal of living in retirement on an income level that is at least very close to, if not more than, what they knew in the everyday working world. They likely are in their peak earning years as retirement approaches, and the idea of having a reduced standard of living in order to reduce taxes is hardly a goal. Especially not in the earliest years of retirement when you are still relatively active and physically able to do some of the things you dreamed of doing.

Consequently, many people in retirement today find themselves in the same tax bracket they occupied during their working years. Their income has not been greatly reduced, and the tax deductions they knew in their younger years—child care expenses, home mortgages, college loans—have most likely disappeared. Moreover, the taxable RMDs they must now take, bring added taxable income and the prospect of being elevated into an even higher tax bracket, something the Olsons might encounter again when Melissa starts taking RMDs from her 403(b) account.

There is another aspect of retirement taxation the experts seldom bothered to discuss. That is the likelihood that one member of a married couple will live part of their life in the unfamiliar and unwelcomed world of the single taxpayer.

The Widow's Tax

We've already talked about how the tax on qualified retirement accounts will eventually be paid by someone, someday. The IRS doesn't especially care who pays it. If it isn't you—the original owner of the IRA or 401(k)—it will be a surviving spouse or second-generation heirs.

In the case of an inheriting spouse, they may well be in a more difficult tax situation than you are today.

Consider Melissa Olson's potential situation. If Ronnie passes before her—as most husbands predecease their wives—her income will decrease slightly, but not as much as you might think. She will lose one Social Security check, the smaller of the couple's two. She will likely lose Ronnie's pension, unless he set up payments for a guaranteed period of time that extended beyond his death. The income from the property rental is still there. There also will be taxable income from RMDs on her own 403(b) account.

But now Melissa also inherits any remaining balance on Ronnie's qualified retirement account. The RMDs and the taxes due are now her responsibility. Let's look at what that might do to her annual income and resulting tax consequence.

Let's say Ronnie passes at age 78 after taking six years of RMDs from his qualified account of $650,000. Melissa inherits an account with a remaining balance of, say, $500,000. She is now 76 and her IRS-determined life expectancy factor is 22.0. Her first RMD from Ronnie's account is $22,700 ($500,000 divided by 22.0).

To be sure, Melissa's annual income will be reduced. But she is now a single filer, which isn't half as tax-friendly as the married filing jointly status she enjoyed for years. Melissa, who spent much of her life in the 22 percent tax bracket, may well find herself with taxable income exceeding $88,386, which in 2021 would elevate a single filer into the 24 percent bracket.

Now let's consider what happens when Melissa eventually passes and her tax obligation passes as well to, let's say, her three adult children.

The "kids" will inherit—if their folks so determined—the remaining balance of their parents' qualified accounts. This is a fully taxable inheritance. Each of the inheritors now faces a 10-year window in which they must liquidate their share of the still unpaid taxes. (Gone after the passage of the SECURE Act of 2019 are the good old days when an inherited IRA could be stretched over the lifetime of the inheritor.) How each inheritor draws down their inherited share is up to them. They could take the inherited IRA in a lump sum, incurring one big tax bill in doing so, or stretch it out over the 10-year period. Either way, the tax effectively reduces the amount of the inheritance.

No question, the children of the late Ronnie and Melissa Olson will be thankful for what their parents left them. At the same time, they may quietly wonder why the people they loved didn't do something to lessen the tax obligation they would eventually pass on. Some effective tax planning—such as paying the tax on their qualified accounts during years when tax brackets were lower than they'd been in decades—would have helped the "kids" who now are paying additional taxes during their own top-earning years.

Passing on undrained pools of qualified money doesn't incur just a widow's penalty. There also is something I've come to call the "kiddos penalty." Both the widows and kiddos penalties greatly reduce your 401(k) "net" after taxes.

We'll talk more in a later chapter about ways to drain the taxable pool before someone else is forced to do it. But first let's take a look at another unknown in dealing with taxes at any stage in life. I'm talking about unknown tax rates in the future.

Tax Secret #3	Don't pin yourself in a corner with retirement account required minimum distributions (RMDs).

The IRA and the ARM: What Rate Are You Paying?

I believe it's time to reexamine the IRA. That is, people need to look at their IRAs as they would if they were purchasing an adjustable-rate mortgage (ARM). Let me explain why.

ARMs are structured such that your interest rate goes up incrementally over the passage of time. You could end up paying higher interest on your loan. If you have a $1 million property with an ARM set at 3 percent interest, you know the interest rate is likely going to go up to 4 percent, 5 percent, maybe even 6 percent over time. What do you do? You do what you have to do to pay off that loan as quickly as possible.

The same concept applies to your retirement account, whether it's an IRA, a 401(k), 403(b), or a 457 plan. Your money in the account is not currently being taxed. But eventually the volcano is going to erupt. You are going to encounter Required Minimum Distributions and you'll have to pay taxes on every cent.

There's really a sort of adjustable-rate mortgage against the taxes on that money in your retirement account. By that I mean that you don't know what the tax rate is going to be at that time in retirement when you'll have to start paying taxes on that money. It's worse than an ARM in that you're flying blind.

If you had an ARM on your home and expected the interest rate to increase—thus increasing the costs substantially to pay off your home one day—you'd do everything you could to pay it down as quickly as possible. Why then wouldn't you do the same with the yet-to-be taxed money in your retirement accounts? Pay it down while tax rates are low.

I can tell you what the tax rate is today, or what it was two years ago. But if you ask me what it will be two years from now, or after December 31, 2025, when the Trump tax cuts are scheduled to sunset, I can't tell you. What I can say is, it will very likely be higher than it is today. My bet, much, much higher.

I say this primarily because of our ever-increasing national debt and what it will take to pay it down.

We've talked about the national debt for years and how it's become a huge problem. Yet every election cycle, what do the politicians do? They talk about increasing benefits, socializing medicine, increasing military spending and piling more debt on top of what we already have.

After World War II, there was a large national debt. What did the politicians do then? They focused on paying it down. They didn't increase expenses; they reduced them. They eventually brought the national debt down, and one of the ways they did that was by raising tax rates. They taxed more people at a higher rate and collected more revenue to help reduce the debt. We haven't done that yet with our current debt, which has only grown larger since the postwar days when it was reduced to a more reasonable level.

That debt exploded to record levels recently because of what economists call a "black swan event," something that couldn't be predicted but can change the economic outlook in the wink of an eye.

We're talking here about the COVID pandemic that erupted in 2020. The resulting quarantines, closed businesses, lost jobs and lost lives put America and the world into an economic tailspin. In an attempt to help American businesses and citizens deal with the economic hardships, Congress in 2020 and 2021 approved stimulus spending programs that added some $4 trillion to the national debt within a matter of months.

On January 1, 2020, America had a GDP that approximately matched our level of national debt. By late 2021, however, that debt was 140 percent of the total of all the goods and services produced here.

Eventually America will have to get serious about bringing down this debt, just as it did in the years after World War II. That's why I believe it's no longer a matter of whether tax rates will go up. It's a matter of *when* they will go up.

Just like interest rates on an adjustable-rate mortgage, income earners as well inheritors should be thinking about the direction in which their taxes are going. And if you're invested in an IRS-approved retirement savings plan—as many Americans are—and you are waiting to pay the taxes that you or someone you love will eventually have to pay, you will very likely end up paying more in taxes just as surely as you will pay more in interest if you wait to pay off a mortgage.

Now, could tax rates go lower? Sure. But that's highly unlikely in today's economic environment. What is more likely is that they will go higher for the reasons already mentioned. The challenge in dealing with that future involves taking action today, and we'll talk about ways of doing just that in an upcoming chapter.

Tax Secret #4	The government doesn't care about your net worth, only how your income hits your tax return.

What You Earn Matters More Than What You Own

There is one final misconception to clear up before closing this chapter on mistaken assumptions about taxation.

Many Americans believe that people of higher net worth should pay higher taxes. A lot of people got upset, for example, when they learned that Donald Trump paid less income tax than they did, largely through his use of depreciation, real estate write-offs, and other tax advantages that high net worth individuals enjoy.

But the truth is, the IRS cares very little about your net worth. All it cares about is how different kinds of taxable income hit your 1040 every year. Among them:

1. How much were your wages, pensions, Social Security, self-employment income?
2. What were your stock dividends and how much interest did you earn on your investments for the year?

3. Did you sell land, investments, or a business? Are the gains long-term or short-term? Do you have losses that offset some or all of the gains?
4. Do you have rental income?
5. Did you take money from your tax-deferred retirement accounts?

These are the things the IRS cares about. It adds up all of your income line items, then deducts your standard and/or itemized deductions and credits to determine your taxable income. When it all comes out of the wash, you could find yourself as a middle-income earner who pays taxes at a higher rate than the billionaires who have access to deductions and credits—to say nothing of having tax lawyers and top-rated accountants—that are not available to everyday Americans. Moreover, a lot of middle-class Americans get hurt more than those of little means or those living high on the hog. The IRS cares more about what is on your tax return than what is actually in your bank account.

And here's the rub. The IRS actually decides much of what appears on that tax form. It determines the standard deduction, or what counts as an itemized deduction. It determines everything from how tips are taxed to how child care is credited.

The IRS influence on your qualified retirement accounts is especially significant. It determines how much in pretax contributions you can make in a year. It determines when and how much you must withdraw from those accounts, as well as what the tax rate will be at the time of doing so. And when the government is making all these decisions, you are on a government retirement program and not your own.

It's your choice. Follow a plan that a government decides for you, or plan your own future.

The challenge is to take more control over your own taxes. Again, the key to doing that is paying off the taxes you must pay eventually at the most tax opportune time available. Specifically, at times such as the years after the Tax Cuts and Jobs Act of 2017 reduced tax rates to some of the lowest levels in more than 40 years. And since the current tax brackets have a shelf life, people facing retirement in a few years should be taking action now to lower their taxes in retirement.

One of the biggest indicators of successful retirement investing is how well you manage your taxes. The impact of taxes on your retirement savings, along with the impact of likely higher future tax rates, will greatly influence your true after-tax spending power and the ultimate success of your retirement planning. This is especially true if you end up in a higher tax bracket at retirement.

The key, again, is to take control of your taxes now, to work to reduce your pool of tax-deferred money while taxes are relatively low. No one can predict how long they might remain this way, but in light of rising national debt, I feel comfortable saying this.

Trust me, a tax hurricane is coming. This is no grand illusion.

CHAPTER 3

Social Security

If you could maintain your lifestyle on Social Security income alone, you might never file another tax return in retirement. Yes, you read that correctly. The IRS considers Social Security benefits to be 100 percent tax-free *if* not accompanied by other sources of income.

But that's a mighty big "if."

OK, I can guess what you're thinking at this point. How many people, you ask rhetorically, can get by on Social Security alone? Well, not many, but some do. The Social Security Administration, in a 2017 survey, found that just under 20 percent of Americans aged 65 and older received at least 90 percent of all income from Social Security. But trying to live on Social Security alone is a tough, tough way to go through retirement, and that isn't what I'm suggesting here. Not at all.

Many readers of this book have additional sources of taxable retirement income from pensions, interest and dividends, rental payments and, most commonly, distributions from tax-deferred accounts. It's that last income component that holds the key to receiving tax-free Social Security benefits.

We'll talk later in this chapter, and elsewhere in this book, about ways of building up a tax-free retirement account, the best known of which is the Roth IRA. Why is this important? Because people who put most or all of their retirement savings into a tax-free account, either through contributions during their working years or through conversions later in life, can take tax-free distributions during retirement that will not be part of their annual tax return. And without additional taxable income on their 1040, they will most likely pay no taxes on Social Security benefits. And, in some cases, they could end up owing no federal taxes at all.

Social Security, to be sure, is a big part of most people's retirement income picture. Accordingly, we'll take an in-depth look at the program in this chapter. We'll first look at the history of Social Security to understand how it grew into what it is today, then get into the basics of how it functions and is taxed.

The History of Social Security

It will come as a surprise to some people to learn that Social Security is taxed at all. After all, haven't we already had a "Social Security tax" withheld from our paychecks throughout our years of employment?

Well, yes, we did. But to understand how this all came about, it's important to understand the evolution of Social Security.

President Franklin Roosevelt signed the Social Security Act in 1935 as one way of dealing with the Great Depression. One of the main goals of the legislation then, as it is today, was to provide a retirement support system for Americans, something that didn't exist in 1935 when pensions were unheard of for all but a few fortunate people.

The legislation also effectively served as a kind of jobs creation act. To understand why, you have to understand the troubled conditions of the time.

Amid the joblessness and breadlines of the 1930s, workers in their late 50s or 60s who were fortunate to still have a job did everything they could to keep it. My grandfather, who worked at a creamery in Northern Minnesota, went to work many days with a broken leg. He did so knowing that if he skipped a day, there was a long list of desperate unemployed workers who would have gladly taken his job. He never even went to the doctor, but he always went to work.

In an effort to open up jobs for unemployed younger workers with young families, Congress passed the Social Security Act. It did so, in part, hoping to induce older workers to retire, knowing they could finally afford to do so with financial support from their government.

The program was not without its detractors, either then or even now.

To fund it, FDR asked American workers to have taxes taken from their paychecks in order to build up what is commonly called the Social Security Trust Fund. As you might guess, workers who were struggling for every penny they could get were not happy to see their money go to support someone else's retirement. Beyond that, what guarantee did they have that this money would be there for them when it came time for their retirement some 20, 30, or 40 years in the future?

Interesting, isn't it, that we still hear those same questions even today?

Keep in mind that very few people in 1935 paid any income tax at all. The income threshold for paying income tax then was $10,000, and most people made nowhere near that much. Only 2.1 percent of Americans filed income tax returns that year, which meant that 98 percent of the country suddenly found taxes being taken out of their paycheck for the first time. It's not hard to understand the early resentment, the anger even, directed toward the program.

To deal with these concerns, Roosevelt got creative. He promised Americans that the government would never tax the Social Security benefits they received in retirement.

That promise lasted until 1983.

How Social Security Came to be Taxed

A lot of things changed in the Social Security program in its first 45 years. More people began using it as more members of the Greatest Generation—the people who survived the Great Depression and won

World War II—began to retire. Additionally, more people also began seeking disability benefits available to those of non-retirement age who were unable to work because of physical affliction. What once was a very solid system—in its earliest years, 40 active workers paid Social Security taxes for every one retiree taking benefits—began showing cracks in its foundation.

I have vague memories of the early concerns people expressed about the long-term viability of Social Security. I was just a second-grader living in Lexington Park, Maryland, one of 10 places we lived before my father retired from the Navy and we moved back to Minnesota. We lived just a short drive from our nation's capital, and our frequent trips to the Smithsonian museums helped me develop a love of history.

I was way too young to understand the concept of federal entitlement programs, but I remember my parents, who had just turned 30, talking worriedly about whether the retirement payments their parents received would be available to them in another 30-some years. The idea that Social Security would not be available to them, the Baby Boomer children of the Greatest Generation, was frightening. That much I understood clearly.

They were talking about it, I later learned, because Jimmy Carter had been talking about it in his successful 1976 presidential campaign against Gerald Ford. (I don't remember all the particulars of their discussion, of course, but I do remember Jimmy Carter vividly. Prior to his election, my grade schoolteacher handed each child a handful of peanuts to plant, just as the soon-to-be-elected president once did as a peanut farmer. My peanuts never did sprout. I still don't know why.)

Concerns about the future of Social Security didn't go away with Carter. For the most part, Boomers have been told since the mid-1970s, early in their careers, to not count on Social Security income for their retirement. Some corrective action needed to be taken. And in 1983, President Ronald Reagan attempted to do so.

In an effort to support the system, Reagan sought and received congressional approval for the first taxes on Social Security benefits.

A threshold based on "provisional income"—which we'll define here shortly—was established, and any Social Security recipient exceeding that threshold would pay tax, at their regular rate, on up to 50 percent of their annual benefits. The first provisional amounts were $25,000 for a single filer, and $32,000 for a couple filing jointly. Keep those levels in mind when we soon consider what they mean in terms of today's dollars.

The bill made it through the legislative process mainly because it was supposed to impact only a small percentage—about 4 percent was the original estimate—of the U.S. population. Most Americans were thinking it would affect others, not themselves.

Ten years later, in 1993, President Bill Clinton signed into law a second tier of Social Security taxation. It established two additional provisional income thresholds—$34,000 for a single filer and $44,000 for a couple filing jointly—above which Social Security recipients would pay tax on up to 85 percent of their annual benefits.

Tax on Social Security: Provisional Income

Filing Status	Provisional Income*	Benefits Subject to Taxation
Married filing jointly	Less than $32,000 >$32,000 - <$44,000 More than $44,000	No benefits taxable Up to 50% of benefits taxable Up to 85% of benefits taxable
Single, Head of Household, Qualifying Widow(er), Married Filing Separately and Living Apart from Spouse	Under $25,000 $25,000 - $34,000 Over $34,000	No benefits taxable Up to 50% of benefits taxable Up to 85% of benefits taxable
Married Filing Separately and Living with Spouse	Over 0	Up to 85% of benefits taxable

*Provisional Income = adjusted gross income (not including Social Security) plus tax-exempt interest plus 50% of Social Security Benefit

So as not to confuse anyone, let's note that retirees are not taxed at a 50 or 85 percent rate. Those rates don't even exist in the current tax code. Rather, up to 50 or 85 percent of their total Social Security benefits are subject to taxation at the filer's regular tax-bracket rate. Example: Bob and Mary Jones reported an annual provisional income of $70,000 on their latest tax return. They were on the upper end of the 12 percent tax bracket in 2021. They both receive Social Security benefits with a combined value of $45,000, meaning their tax on that benefit would be $4,590—12 percent tax on 85 percent of $45,000.

A couple of final notes on thresholds for Social Security taxation.

The numbers used today have never been adjusted by Congress since the passing of the 1983 and 1993 legislation. In nearly 40 years, the calculation numbers have never been adjusted for inflation. In 1983, $32,000 could buy you a cabin in Minnesota. Today, you're lucky to get a used car for that amount. In 1993, imposing higher Social Security taxes on couples making $44,000 a year was considered a tax on higher earnings. It's still a decent income today, but it's hardly considered "wealthy." Inflation changes the value of the income. And yet when people talk about Social Security reform today, you seldom hear discussions about raising provisional income thresholds.

Here's another perspective on the effect of inflation over time. In 1993, when Congress was considering adding a second level of Social Security taxes, the Social Security Administration estimated that only 20 percent of beneficiary families would pay income tax on any part of their benefits. Today, more than half of retirees are paying tax on their Social Security. Wages rose while the taxation thresholds stayed the same. Consequently, more retirees than ever are paying taxes on their hard-earned benefits.

So much for the promise of tax-free retirement income.

What is Provisional Income?

The way provisional income is determined is an important part of the calculation that determines if, or how much of, your Social Security benefit is subject to taxation.

You begin with your adjusted gross income as reported on Form 1040 of your annual tax return. You then add in all tax-free interest from investments. Finally, you add half of the Social Security benefits reported on your Form SSA-1099. This total is your provisional income. If it exceeds the threshold limits of your filing status, you are subject to taxation on up to either 50 or 85 percent of your Social Security income.

Allow me a few personal observations here. Despite dire warnings that the Social Security Trust Fund will incur a negative balance sometime in the 2030s—when persons receiving benefits exceed the number of people paying FICA taxes—I still believe the program will be there for years to come, certainly for readers of this book and their children. But I also believe there will be changes. There may be cutbacks in benefits, an increase in withholding taxes and possibly in the tax on benefits. I personally wouldn't be surprised to see the day when higher earners find 100 percent of their benefits—as opposed to today's top level of 85 percent—are subject to taxation.

The Basics of Social Security

If I could reduce the basics of Social Security down to its most elementary rules, they would be these:

1. You've got to pay to play (or have a spouse who did).
2. You have to be present to win.
3. The longer you wait to collect, the more you stand to win.

The amount of Social Security benefit you will ultimately receive depends on three factors. First, how long you worked and how much you paid into a system that one day will pay you back—if you are still here to collect. Secondly, the total amount of benefits you receive depends on how long you live—a time frame none of us knows. Third, the month and year in which you begin taking benefits set a lifetime baseline for the amount you will receive each month. Really, this is the only element over which we have any real control in what is an otherwise uncertain situation.

Let's look more closely at each of these three "rules."

You've Got to Pay to Play

The Federal Insurance Contributions Act (FICA) requires you to pay 6.2 percent (under 2022 rules) of your gross pay into what is most commonly called the Social Security Trust Fund, along with another 1.45 percent for Medicare. Perhaps it will cheer you up to learn your employer must match those same amounts on your behalf. On a less encouraging note, self-employed people must pay withholding as both an employee and employer, meaning they lay out a full 15.3 percent in FICA taxes.

Your involuntary contributions are pooled with those of all other American workers in the Federal Old Age and Survivors Trust Fund as well as the Federal Disability Insurance Trust Fund.

(Let's note here that for the purposes of this chapter, all discussions of Social Security benefits will be limited to those available through the Old Age and Survivors Trust Fund that you become eligible for at age 62, as opposed to those of the Social Security Disability Insurance [SSDI] aspect of the program.)

The Social Security Trust Fund is managed by the Social Security Administration (SSA). It invests all pooled resources in securities guaranteed by the full faith and credit of the U.S. government. The fund in turn makes regular payments to seniors and persons with disabilities.

Within this huge fund you have your own pool of invested money. It's called your primary insurance amount (PIA), and it's based on your work history and earnings. Your PIA serves as the basis in computing the benefit you will receive at full retirement age (FRA), with your best 35 years of earnings composing that basis.

This doesn't mean you have to work 35 years to collect Social Security. But you do have to amass 40 work "credits" (in SSA parlance) to be eligible for benefits. Most people earn four credits in a typical work year, meaning a 10-year employment history—though not necessarily 10 consecutive years—is necessary to receive benefits.

If you work for, say, 40-plus years (as many people do before retiring), the SSA makes your top-earning 35 years the basis of your PIA. A work history of fewer years simply means a smaller PIA pool. Any missing work years are averaged into the equation as zeros and can substantially reduce your PIA.

Conversely, people who have worked 35 or more years—and I'd suggest that probably includes most people reading this book—have pretty much already topped out their PIA pool. In other words, if you're reading this book at or near age 60 and you've already worked 35 years, you're probably not going to appreciably grow your PIA (and your monthly benefit) with an extra year or two of work. You can, however, increase your benefit by waiting to begin taking Social Security, and we'll discuss this option here shortly.

You can track your Social Security earnings history by registering at www.ssa.gov/mystatement. The secure website will take your personal information and project what your benefit—based on your earnings history at the time you make the inquiry—will be if taken at (1) the earliest possible time, (2) at full retirement age, or (3) even later at age 70.

You Have to Be Present to Win

Social Security has what loosely can be called a "you have to be present to win" rule. This means—with the exception of people with disabilities—you must reach what is generally considered "retirement age" before you can start getting back the money the government has been taking from your paycheck and setting aside for you all these years.

The SSA considers this minimum age to be 62. For a single person who dies before reaching that age and does not have a surviving spouse or minor children—well, thanks for playing the game, as there is no prize for the late, great you. This is not a pleasant thought, but if it happens … you won't be around to care, will you? Nor are you likely to be consoled by the thought that your contributions to the Social Security Trust Fund are much appreciated by the people who benefited from them in the past and will do so in the future. Again, not a pleasant thought, but as my grandfather once told me: People make better decisions when they are brave enough to face their own mortality, and wise enough to plan accordingly.

However, there is a consolation prize for anyone passing before full retirement age who leaves behind a surviving spouse and/or minor children. There are benefits available for surviving spouses, but even widows and widowers have to be at least age 60 (in most cases) before becoming eligible to receive survivor benefits.

(Note: persons interested in learning more about how spousal or survivor benefits are determined can find additional information in Joe Lucey's comprehensive book that explores all aspects of Social Security: *The Retiree's Social Security Guide: Your Blueprint to Maximize Mailbox Income.*)

The Longer You Wait to Collect, the More You Stand to Win

For those still "in the game," 62 is the earliest you can receive your personal benefits, but 62 is not considered full retirement age (FRA). As a result, a reduced benefit is paid to persons who begin taking benefits prior to FRA on the theory that they will ultimately receive more payments over a longer period of time than will those starting benefits at FRA or later.

FRA, which is age 66 or 67 for most readers of this book, is the key to the vast world of Social Security benefits. There are decisions to be made either before, at, or after this date that can reduce or enhance the benefits you can receive. Because of that, you absolutely must know your full retirement age, as indicated in the chart below, in order to make an informed decision on when to begin taking benefits.

FRA determines, among other things, the age at which you will receive your duly-earned full benefit. It also determines how much that benefit will be reduced should you elect to begin taking benefits early—that is, in the years between age 62 and your FRA. A monthly benefit will decrease at slightly more than 6 percent for each full year in which benefits are taken before reaching FRA.

Benefits Vary Based on Age of Retirement

Year of Birth	Full (normal) Retirement Age	Months between age 62 and full retirement age	At Age 62			
			A $1000 retirement benefit would be reduced to	The retirement benefit is reduced by	A $500 spouse's benefit would be reduced to	The spouse's benefit is reduced by
1943-1954	66	48	$750	25.00%	$350	30.00%
1955	66 & 2 months	50	$741	25.83%	$345	30.83%
1956	66 & 4 months	52	$733	26.67%	$341	31.67%
1957	66 & 6 months	54	$725	27.50%	$337	32.50%
1958	66 & 8 months	56	$716	28.33%	$333	33.33%
1959	66 & 10 months	58	$708	29.17%	$329	34.17%
1960 and later	67	60	$700	30.00%	$325	35.00%

Source: "Retirement Benefits: Starting Your Retirement Early" www.ssa.gov/benefits

FRA also determines how much your benefit will be enhanced should you choose to delay taking benefits until sometime after reaching FRA. Delayed retirement credits can increase a monthly benefit by 8 percent for each full year between FRA and age 70, the age at which delayed retirement credits end.

We noted previously, but it bears repeating, that the monthly benefit you receive upon first taking benefits establishes a baseline that stays with you for the rest of your life. Only annual cost-of-living adjustments (COLAs), determined by the SSA and based on the rate of inflation, can increase the established baseline.

FRA is also a key number when determining survivor and spousal benefits, as well as the age at which there are no restrictions on wages earned while receiving Social Security.

FRA has been a sliding number over its history. When Social Security first began as a Depression Era program, age 65 was considered retirement age. But as time went on and life expectancies increased with advances in medicine and healthier lifestyles, it soon became obvious that Social Security was supporting retired people who were living longer than folks did in the 1930s.

The government consequently implemented a sliding scale that gradually increased FRA. For the majority of Baby Boomers born from 1943 through 1954, FRA became age 66. Legislation that took effect in 2000 increased the FRA to age 67 for persons born in 1960 and later. A sliding scale exists for persons born between 1955 and 1959, with FRA ranging from 66 years and 2 months to 66 years and 10 months, respectively.

Bottom Line: Watch Your Retirement Income

The key to retiring well is to have your Social Security benefits pay for your lifestyle. That doesn't mean you have to tighten your belt and reduce your expenses to some amount below your monthly Social Security income. That's not what I'm saying.

Retirement should be a period of abundance. You shouldn't have to watch your income, your checkbook, and your budget like you did when your kids were in diapers and you were trying to figure out whether you could replace the bald tires on your car. That shouldn't be what retirement is about.

At the same time, though, keep in mind that Social Security income is taxed only when other sources of income hit the tax return. Again, the IRS doesn't care what your net worth is. It only cares about your income. So, you need to keep an eye on wages or additional income you receive, including dividends, interest, capital gains, rental income, and distributions. All of your taxable income sources count in determining how much (if any) of your benefits will be taxed.

Unless, that is, you take action—preferably in the years before retirement—to reduce or eliminate that taxable income, especially the pool of tax-deferred money in your IRA, 401(k), or other qualified retirement savings program.

Remember, this is money you will be required to pay taxes on someday. For most readers of this book, that time comes when you reach age 72 and must begin taking fully taxable Required Minimum Distributions from your qualified accounts. These distributions, whether needed or not, will increase both taxable income and provisional income, thus affecting the tax on your Social Security benefits.

But by using tax strategies such as those we employ in our Tax-Smart™ planning program, a person can begin paying the inevitable taxes on qualified money at more tax-opportune times. Specifically, times such as today when tax rates are as low as they've been in 40 years. Paying taxes at discount rates can greatly reduce or even eliminate the taxes that will show up on your 1040 in retirement. By lowering provisional income to below the threshold for Social Security taxation, it's possible for people to live on Social Security benefits and distributions from a tax-free account such as a Roth IRA while paying reduced or even no federal income tax at all.

That's the strategy for optimizing your taxes in retirement. It's the biggest secret surrounding Social Security benefits and the taxes associated with those benefits. If you get your total income from all sources below the threshold of taxable income, then you can live your retirement years without paying any federal income tax. That's what I want to help you do.

Tax Secret #5	Don't underestimate your Social Security election decision. Get advice on how you can best optimize your Social Security benefits to make them tax efficient.

CHAPTER 4

IRAs and Tax Traps

A government retirement plan tells you what you can do with your own money. It tells you when to start liquidating, how much tax to pay on it and when, and how to design a retirement around it. In a sense, it's a tax trap.

I covered much of this in a previous chapter, but a little review wouldn't hurt.

The Biggest Tax Trap of Them All

A misguided assumption we've been told (and came to believe) over the last 30 years is that you can put money into a retirement account, get an immediate tax deduction, and have that money grow tax-deferred. Nothing wrong to this point. But we were also told that when you're ready to take your money out of that account, you'll be in a lower tax bracket. The problem is, there are 10,000 Baby Boomers retiring every month and finding out that's not always the case.

Many Baby Boomers are actually paying more in taxes when they take their money out of their retirement accounts.

Tax-deferred does not mean the same thing as tax-free. People are told (correctly) that these traditional IRAs and similar investment vehicles are tax-deferred. But they are lulled into thinking these are "tax-free" because they're not paying taxes right now. The taxes are essentially invisible until they show up 20, 30, or 40 years later in retirement.

I am not suggesting that contributing to a tax-deferred account is the wrong thing to do, but understand that these accounts can be a double-edged sword. The ability to grow these accounts is a tremendous opportunity. But be cautious of the bottom part of the blade and begin planning early to ensure that your tax savings today don't end up cutting deep as you take your balances out in your retirement.

People want to do the right thing. They start putting money into their retirement accounts as soon as they can, and put as much money into those accounts while they can. What's happening is, they're sacrificing money they could have been using for other things like taking the kids to Disneyland or buying a new car. Their retirement accounts can grow to have large sums of money in them, but those accounts are not *individual* retirement accounts, which is what "IRA" stands for. We actually have a joint partner in them.

Your joint partner is the IRS, which has a say in how much money you actually get when you take it out. They have an interest in that account.

Whether you have $250,000, $1 million, or $10 million in your retirement account, you've got to realize that it's not all your money. Remember, you've got a "mortgage" on that money in that either you or an inheritor of your account will have to pay tax on it eventually. And since you don't know what your future tax rate will be, you need to plan as if you expect it to go up.

If you're 40 years old right now, based on current law, you'll have to start taking money out of your IRA at age 72. It used to be 70½ years old, but the starting age went up when Congress passed the SECURE Act in December 2019 and President Trump signed it into law.

SECURE is an acronym that stands for Setting Every Community Up for Retirement Enhancement. I believe, and most readers probably realize this, that whenever Congress refers to legislation as "SECURE," it's time to put your hand on your wallet and slowly back away.

The SECURE Act is a misnomer. It raised the age at which you must start taking money out of your retirement account to 72. But many families might not need this money at that age. It could be money you would not ordinarily use because you have other sources of income. That's hardly an "enhancement."

We've been trained to grow our money in tax-deferred status; then we're forced to take that money out of our retirement account at a certain time whether we need it or not. On top of that, you're taxed on that money when you take it out no matter what tax bracket you fall into. This causes some families to end up paying taxes on Social Security income that might not otherwise be taxable. Others may even be pushed into a higher tax bracket or forced to pay higher Medicare premiums, as happened to the Olsons in the previous chapter. It's a round-robin tax trap that can bite you multiple times. It's like falling into a snake pit.

Meet Your Retirement Partner, the IRS

The best way to think about your IRA, 401(k), and other qualified retirement accounts is to consider them a partnership between you and the IRS. Think about how much of that money is going to you and how much is going to Uncle Sam. The reality is, it's anybody's guess how much the IRS is going to get.

The reason we don't know how much belongs to the IRS is that tax laws change. It's extremely likely that they'll change in 20 years. It's also possible that they'll change in five or even 10 years. Your tax rate could go up or down, but I'm betting it will likely go up due to previously cited reasons such as COVID-19 shutdowns that led to a temporary economic decline, trillions in stimulus spending, and increased government debt.

A likely increase in federal taxes is one thing. But now let's also factor in the effect of state and local taxes as well.

If you live in Minnesota and your federal income tax rate is 22 percent, the state will add about 6.8 percent to that amount. Adding these figures together means your effective tax rate is nearly 29 percent. It's called the "marginal" tax rate. You can figure your marginal tax rate for your current state residency in a similar fashion.

Higher earners in Minnesota (as well as other places with state and local taxes) can easily find themselves nearing the 42 percent marginal tax rate (32 percent federal tax bracket plus 9.8 percent in state and local taxes). Let's take a look at what that does to the spending power of the money in your qualified retirement account.

The bottom line on your quarterly IRA or 401(k) statement may show $1 million, and you feel pretty good about that (as you should). But you also must remember that not all of this money is yours. Uncle Sam also has a stake, a 32 percent claim (as much as $320,000) in the above example. In addition, the money you are required to take from this account beginning at age 72 adds to your taxable income, thus creating a bigger piece of the pie from which your state or local taxing authority can take a bigger bite. The true spending power of the $1 million you've saved over the years is considerably less than you imagined.

Right now, tax rates are the lowest they've been in 40 years. That means if you start voluntarily liquidating your IRA now—before the government requires you to do so—you'll pay taxes at a lower rate than you would have a decade ago, or very likely a decade from now. If taxes go up in five years and you start liquidating your IRA then, you'll pay more in taxes at that time. By waiting to pay taxes only when you are required to do so, you're guessing about what the tax rate is going to be in the future. It's a gamble. So which path are you going to gamble on?

This much we know for certain. At the end of December 2025, the Tax Cuts and Jobs Act of 2017 is scheduled to expire. If Congress does nothing to extend this "sunset" provision, your taxes will go up—reverting to the higher levels of 2017—on January 1, 2026. They could go up even sooner, as President Joe Biden came into office in 2021 talking about raising taxes on the "rich," a level he defined as income of over $400,000. But given the historically upward trend of taxes, I personally wouldn't be surprised if there wasn't also some increase for most Americans.

Many people are going to be caught unaware. When they start preparing their taxes for the 2026 tax year, they are likely to see their taxes go up. They may find themselves in a higher tax bracket. If they're retired and collecting Social Security, they may find themselves suddenly paying tax on those benefits and possibly paying higher Medicare premiums. Their capital gains taxes could go up too, or their other government benefits could get reduced. In other words, we're sitting on a tax time bomb.

There's your tax trap.

Tax Secret #6	Move your money away from tax-deferred retirement accounts to take advantage of today's low taxes rather than wait until you retire to pay taxes when they will likely be higher.

The Inheritance Tax Trap

Some Americans are under the mistaken impression that they can avoid paying the inevitable taxes on their qualified retirement accounts by passing that money to someone else.

If only.

If you think you can transfer that retirement account to your spouse while you're alive, think again. You can't give it to your wife as if it's a house, a stock certificate, or another asset. If you transfer it, you'll create a taxable event that requires you to pay taxes on it immediately. That makes it a tax trap in a completely different sense.

As noted previously, every penny of your tax-deferred money, no matter where it sits, is going to be taxed eventually. The question is, when? And, by whom?

To repeat an important point made previously, any spouse inheriting the untaxed balance of a qualified retirement account must pay taxes on that money when distributions are taken, either voluntarily or required. In a similar vein, non-spousal inheritors also incur the tax obligation, but this one comes with a deadline. The passage of the SECURE Act now requires non-spousal inheritors to liquidate an inherited retirement account—and pay its tax bill—within a 10-year period.

How might a person remove this tax obligation from a surviving spouse or other cherished inheritors?

The key is in draining the pool of qualified money at the most opportune time, preferably while they're still here to do so. And the best time to drain that pool and pay those taxes is when taxes are low.

The key is to move your money when it makes the most sense for your financial situation. If it's in a tax-deferred account now and you expect taxes to go up in the future, then now is better than later for paying taxes. If you leave your tax-deferred retirement account to your spouse or other loved ones, then they will end up paying taxes on it at that future tax rate.

All around, this government-sponsored retirement account is a tax trap, any way you look at it.

CHAPTER 5

Create Your Plan Before the Crisis

There is a huge difference between reactive investment plans and proactive income and tax-efficient planning. Your goal should be to maximize your tax-efficient income, but you need a strategy now.

When you have a plan in place and time on your side—specifically, time before the tax hurricane hits—you can think more clearly about your current situation, goals, and objectives. But if you wait until the storm is on you before you think about contingencies, it's too late. You'll likely jump into crisis mode and look like a drowning person flailing their arms and crying out for help.

People with forward-looking tax and income plans tend to do better in times of uncertainty. When the coronavirus came along in early 2020, for instance, the market fell 37 percent within a few short weeks. Some investors were swamped by the downturn. But families that had a written income plan detailing where their money would come from, and how they would have enough to live on during a crisis event, stood a better chance of surviving the financial storm intact. The impact of the downturn was less devastating to them and they could sleep easier at night knowing they weren't just "winging it." Their plan, not the crisis, was in control.

The military develops such action plans long before they go into combat. They practice, repeat, practice, repeat, practice and repeat all possible scenarios so that they know what to do when they come under fire. Police SWAT teams do the same. Football teams spend most of each practice session going through situations they are likely to face at game time. They want to be ready for anything, so they plan for the unpredictable.

You have to think about your retirement plan the same way.

What will you do when financial uncertainty comes? You need a plan right now that outlines how you will handle a market downturn, or an unexpected event such as a medical emergency or temporary unemployment. You need a plan that lays out what you can do before an impending tax hike. You need a plan that details how you will pay down your taxes or move your money around in order to avoid unnecessary tax increases. You need this plan to be customized to your unique financial situation, and you need it documented so it can be referenced when you need it. You also need to review this plan often, to mentally rehearse how you will react during times of uncertainty. The time to do all this is when conditions are stable and predictable, long before the storm appears on the horizon.

Don't Underestimate Inflation

Don't forget, either, that your plan also must adjust for inflation, something many people tended to overlook until the post-pandemic years.

That's probably because inflation had been relatively tame in the current century, having exceeded 3 percent or more annually only six times from 2000 through 2020.[15] Things were even calmer since 2012 when annual inflation exceeded 2 percent only four times.

But in 2021, as America and the world seemed to be emerging from the COVID-19 pandemic that brought many economic activities to a halt the previous year, inflation reminded us of the ugly impact

---

[15]"Historical Inflation Rates, 2014–2022." www.usinflationcalculator.com

it can have on the consumer's pocketbook. It rose 4.7 percent on an annual basis in 2021, and its year-over-year increase topped 6 percent in the year's final three months. By January 2022, prices, as measured by the Consumer Price Index, rose 7.5 percent when compared to January 2021—the highest rise in 40 years. Price hikes initially felt mainly in building supplies, microchips, and automobiles (new and used) were soon stinging consumers at neighborhood grocery stores, gas pumps, and seemingly everywhere else they looked.

The lesson to be learned here is that a retirement plan that doesn't adjust for inflation is an incomplete plan, at best.

On my radio programs, I often use an analogy I like to describe inflation. It's been said that when a frog is immersed in boiling water, it will do everything it can to escape. But when the frog is immersed in only slightly warm water, it likes the surroundings, thinks it's in a bath or back home in the swamp. You can gradually turn the heat up to a boiling point and eventually produce, well, frog soup.

Inflation creeps up on us much the same way. What starts out as a warm bath suddenly gets hot enough to scald, often without our realizing it. It's no wonder Ronald Reagan called inflation the "silent killer" of retirement savings plans.

Similarly, you shouldn't wait until your taxes are boiling over before deciding to do something to lower the heat.

When it comes time to make tax decisions, you need to know where you stand within your current tax bracket long before decision time is upon you. Are you in the lower, middle or upper range of that bracket? This is important to know in order to have an idea about how much money you can move around from, say, a tax-deferred IRA into a tax-free Roth IRA without incurring income that elevates you into a higher tax bracket.

Yes, you will pay tax on any funds converted in this manner. But if you have the chance to pay that inevitable tax bill when rates are lower and make conversions without affecting your current tax rate, you can minimize your future taxes that are likely to arrive at an even higher rate. This is part of what real tax planning is about.

Crises are going to happen. Earthquakes, infrastructure failure, financial calamity; it happens. Job loss, death in the family—there is always something that will throw you off-kilter. Those who are prepared handle it better when it happens. During the pandemic, for instance, businesses that planned with continuity testing fared better than those that didn't.

When we think about taxes, we should always be prepared for the likely event that they will go higher. When they do, we should be prepared financially for that happening. Make a plan so that any increase doesn't take us by surprise and put us in a crisis situation. The idea is to avoid surprise and crisis, as bad decisions often are made in the midst of chaos.

A half hour of planning with a TaxSmart™ financial advisor can pinpoint five to 10 different crisis situations for which you need to prepare. Then, when another market downturn happens, you can spend your time following your plan and responding to the event based on how you prepared for it. Even if such an event never occurs, you'll have peace of mind knowing that you were protected, similar to the reasons you buy any type of insurance.

Yet, according to Charles Schwab, only 25 percent of Americans have a financial plan. And among those who do, many don't have a written policy or procedures for how much risk they should take with their investments.

Tax Secret #7	Create your tax and income plan before a crisis.

Handling Risk in Retirement

I believe there are three types of retirement investment risks that everyone needs to consider in their financial planning:

1. **Inflation risk** – This involves the chance that inflation will eat away at your returns if your investments don't earn enough to keep up with inflation. This can happen when your portfolio is weighted too heavily toward conservative investments with low rates of return. Inflation is another thing that is hard to predict, and it fluctuates. We don't know the inflation rate until after the fact when we compare wages and prices year over year. Every investment portfolio needs to outpace inflation, and investments earning only 1 or 2 percent returns aren't likely to do that.

2. **Risk capacity** – Risk capacity is a mathematical model that calculates the minimum balance necessary in all of your retirement savings accounts to enable ongoing withdrawals for income and expenses (known or unknown) so that you do not run out of money in retirement.

3. **Risk tolerance** – Risk tolerance has to do with your emotions. People with a high-risk tolerance typically make riskier investments than do their low-risk counterparts. They might well absorb more losses in a market downturn before reaching the panic threshold that prompts emotional decisions, many of which are counterintuitive to what one would normally do.

A word of caution here: Be careful not to confuse risk capacity with risk tolerance. Just because someone has a high propensity to accept risk with their investments does not necessarily mean they have the capacity to accept losses.

Let's consider an example that illustrates the difference.

Imagine a retiree whose income is $100,000 a year from pensions and Social Security but who spends only $60,000 a year. Let's compare this person to a retiree with $100,000 in income but who spends $200,000 annually maintaining their lifestyle. While both have the same income, the first has a much higher risk capacity as they need no withdrawals from savings to maintain their standard of living. The second retiree, however, must tap into savings each year to maintain their lifestyle. This person has very little risk capacity.

Let's consider another example. On one hand we have a gambler who is always at the track betting on the ponies or visiting the sportsbooks. He places large bets to "hit the big one," but often falls short in covering essential living expenses like his mortgage. He has high risk tolerance, yet low risk capacity.

On the flip side is the laborer who never had a high-paying job, never invested in anything more speculative than a bank certificate of deposit or U. S. Treasury Savings Bonds. He maintained a "frugal" standard of living and died with a nice amount of money in the bank. His risk tolerance was nonexistent, but due to his very conservative standard of living, he certainly had a higher risk capacity.

The gambler who risks it all and the laborer who avoids risk at all costs could both be accused of being poor stewards of money. They both allow the thrill of risk or the fear of loss to control their emotions.

Both could have improved their risk capacity by increasing their retirement "mailbox income," which is money that hits your bank account on a regular basis no matter what is going on with the stock market and your retirement accounts. These regular payments include Social Security, pensions, rental income, dividends and interest, annuity payments, and any other income you receive regularly each month. Creating more of this "sustainable income" can put you in a better position to weather the inevitable storm of market ups and downs. Let's look at why I believe this.

As noted above, in March and April of 2020, COVID-related quarantines and business shutdowns caused the market to tumble some 37 percent in a matter of weeks. Many investors with low risk tolerance bailed out quickly, and eventually even some higher risk-tolerant people also headed for the exits. In doing so, they all violated the "buy low, sell high" investment philosophy they believed in, but the sudden plunge of all major market indexes—an event that made many recall the tumble that started the Great Recession in 2008—put many in crisis mode and induced a wave of panic selling.

It didn't have to be that way.

People who had a detailed income plan—people who knew they could depend on reliable sources of mailbox income free from market risk—were in a better position to ride out what eventually proved to be the shortest bear market in history. Instead of selling stock shares at lower prices in a panic mode, these investors were able to "hold the line" or even do some selective buying when stocks were at discount prices. They could afford to wait for the rebound of a market that reached record levels just several months later.

Risk Management Is Emotion Management

When it comes to risk tolerance, some families are taking on more or less risk than they should. And many have no real idea of the risk level they are exposed to.

Some are like the gambler we just met, the guy at the horse track every day. He keeps betting on the ponies—his emotions telling him he's due to hit "the Big One"—but he may well have nothing in savings and is living paycheck to paycheck. Every month, he tosses his sofa cushions trying to figure out where his next meal is coming from. If an income windfall should arrive—whether through wages or welfare or a winning bet on a longshot horse—he quickly heads back to the track to gamble money he can't afford to lose. He has a high risk tolerance but a low risk capacity and often little to show for the risks taken. (I'd also suggest he doesn't have much horse sense.)

This is how some people approach their retirement investments. They can't afford to lose money, but they're gambling it anyway. They don't think they're gambling, but they may not realize the level of risk involved with their investments. When we show what they could lose versus how much they can afford to lose, their eyes get big. Yet some continue to take on more risk thinking it's the right thing to do.

On the other extreme, there are those with very low risk tolerance. They won't buy so much as a church raffle ticket, let alone sit at a casino table or bet on the ponies. They prefer to keep their money close to the vest, "safe" in savings accounts or CDs. There are no major ups and downs in their account balance, yet they see their savings slowly, painfully trickle away over time due to the loss of buying power caused by inflation, something their passbook savings struggle to keep up with.

Clearly, each individual retirement investor is different, yet all have something in common. That is, the need to manage risk in their retirement savings. The key to doing so, I believe, is to consider all three risk elements when developing a plan. To be more specific, you need to consider:

- What kind of risk do you think you can take (tolerance)?
- What kind of risk can you afford to take (capacity)?
- And finally, will your retirement savings outpace inflation?

Unfortunately, some elements of the financial industry tend to focus entirely on risk tolerance while ignoring the other two. For example:

Once a year, when your company's 401(k) representative comes out to talk about your retirement plan, they are likely to include some discussion about the risk you are willing to take in the investments you make within that plan. They will likely present you with a 10- to 20-question survey designed to determine whether you are an aggressive, moderate, or conservative investor. But the reality is, even if the survey gets it right (which it rarely does), it's only looking at one-third of the risk equation.

There are several problems with focusing only on risk tolerance.

One involves an emotional factor I call "recency." Here's what I mean by that.

If you fill out a questionnaire when the market is doing well, you might indicate that you are an aggressive investor, especially if you've recently moved your money into aggressive accounts during recent upward market trends. But in a different kind of market, such as a temporary downturn, you might well answer those same questions differently. The idea of "recency" suggests that your evaluation of your risk tolerance is influenced most by current events, and that this outlook may not be an accurate reflection of what you truly believe about yourself.

In the market correction of 2020, many Americans saw their investment portfolios take a significant hit. It scared them. Now ask yourself: Would their answers on a risk tolerance survey taken then be the same as those on the same survey taken several months later when the market was reaching record level several times a month?

If you're focused only on one-third of the risk equation, you're making an incomplete evaluation of your personal situation. You've no doubt heard the expression, "Garbage in, garbage out?" Your risk assessment may suggest that you're ready to enter the lions' den, but things start looking very different when the big cats begin to roar. Suddenly, a comfortable seat on the stands starts looking pretty good.

To repeat a point made previously, but one that cannot be emphasized enough:

The best way to mitigate your risk is to have a planning-first mentality. First, meet with a financial professional and develop a retirement plan that ensures you always have the income you need regardless of market performance. Second, reduce your taxable footprint. Keeping more of your money in your own pocket is just one way of increasing risk capacity. And finally, plan to grow assets you may need for future retirement costs—long-term care, for example—at whatever risk level you are comfortable with and can afford.

The time to act is now before the hurricane hits. It's the time to make cool-headed decisions based on logic rather than emotion. People tend to think logically … right up until they get hit by flying debris or the house crashes in around them. Then things get emotional, and that's a bad place from which to try to make good decisions.

Emotion just gets in the way of good decision-making. It makes us act in ways we don't want to act. Emotion is why we sometimes lash out at our children when they do or say something they shouldn't, or at a pet who messed on the carpet. It's only later that we realize we shouldn't have been so harsh. Sure, we were angry at the time, but that doesn't mean we don't love the kids any less. And the rug can be cleaned or even replaced, something that can't be said about the love of children or a pet.

A major part of any financial plan is to remove this emotion. This is especially true in retirement planning. A properly developed plan—one that provides income for life, which reduces taxes and considers all elements of risk in the future growth of assets—can remove much of the anxiety people feel when market downturns adversely affect the investments upon which they depend for essential income. That should be the goal of any plan.

CHAPTER 6

Tax Control: Don't Run with the Herd

Most mornings, I stop by my local Starbucks on the way to the office and grab a $3.17 Venti dark roast coffee, no sugar, no cream: just a good black and bitter coffee. My wife makes fun of me because the coffee at the office is just as good for a fraction of the cost. In fact, I rarely finish the drink on the way in, often only having a sip or two during the short drive. But a little gift to myself every morning is a part of my routine, and I enjoy the treat.

Recently, I arrived at the window to pay for my little extravagance and the barista informed me that the car in front of me "paid it forward" by paying for my drink. *Wow, how nice*, I thought to myself, *I'll return the favor and pay it forward to the car behind me.* But I should have looked first because behind me was a car packed with teenage cheerleaders. You guessed it, they all ordered large mocha latte such and suches and my $3 drink self-treat turned into a $25 gesture of blind niceness.

Looking back, I'd do it over again, but I thought this story might illustrate my next point very well. You see, all too often we invest in ways we feel are appropriate but end up paying forward for someone else's tax benefit. One way I've seen this happen most often in my nearly 30 years in financial services is with mutual funds. Investing in the wrong kind of accounts could cause us to end up paying for someone else's tax benefit.

Let me explain.

You've likely been told to buy low and sell high. Successful investors do that more often than buying high and selling low. If they didn't, they'd lose money.

It's like a magic formula. It doesn't matter what grand wizard came up with it if all the other wizards do it and it works. I've heard people attribute the following bit of wisdom to Warren Buffett. Others say it was one of the Rothschilds. Maybe it was JP Morgan. Whoever it was, somebody once said that the Number 1 rule of retirement planning is to never lose money. The Number 2 rule: never forget rule Number 1.

Intuitively, we know this to be true. One key to doing this involves controlling one's emotions when making investment decisions. That's easier said than done, however, when the emotions of "the herd" are involved.

Let's Talk about Mutual Funds

Before 1924, if you wanted to invest in the stock market, you had one option. You went to a broker who created a transaction for you, and you paid a commission fee on that transaction. Because of this arduous process, and the cost involved, few families owned stocks. My dad was the first person in our family to buy a stock, and he was born in the 1940s. Up to that point, most families were like mine. They didn't own stocks.

But then Massachusetts Investors' Trust (today known as MFS Investment Management) came up with a concept to get more people to invest. They created this product that would allow investors to pool their money together. You'd put in $100, I'd put in $100, and several other people would put in $100. It would all go into one account and we'd hire somebody to buy and sell stocks on our behalf. That was how the mutual fund was created.

What this new investment product did was change the landscape of investing forever. Another change, the creation of the IRA, came about much later and also had a huge impact on the number of people who could invest. Before the IRA, however, mutual funds were revolutionary.

The challenge for the manager of this pooled money was to buy investments at a low price and sell them at a higher price, thus increasing the value of the fund for the pooled investors. Those investments existed in three broad categories: stocks, bonds, and cash. Stocks (or equities) consisted of ownership in companies. Bonds, or fixed-income assets, consisted of loans made to big companies.

Portfolio managers were evaluated on two criteria. First, they were evaluated on how well they could manage a portfolio against a certain industry-benchmark. Secondly, they were evaluated based on how well they could manage cash, which became huge profit centers for mutual fund companies.

Here's a scenario: Let's say you sent $1,000 to Joe Lucey to put into the Joe Lucey Mutual Fund. I would take that money and initially put it into a cash account. I wouldn't buy anything right away because that cash is really important. First, it's held for moments of opportunity that allow the fund manager to invest in the right deals. These are opportunities where Joe Lucey can buy low and sell later at a higher price. These might be stock opportunities, bond opportunities, real estate, or whatever that mutual fund happened to be focused on.

Another reason cash is important is for paying redemptions. When investors agree to put their money into the pool, the mutual fund manager agrees to send their money back to them upon request. No delay. The cash account allows the fund manager to have certain liquid assets available to meet those demands. He doesn't need to sell something to fulfill the request.

Let's say our fund manager is doing a really good job. He or she bought a large block of Nozama, a fictional name for a prominent stock that is the largest holding in the fund, at $2,000 a share. Now, it's over $3,000. Good, right? And because the fund has yet to sell any of its Nozama stock, fund participants are not yet paying any tax on its gains.

(We need to note here that the value of the Nozama stock is only a part of the calculation used to determine the net asset value [NAV] of the mutual fund when it is bought or sold. The fund's NAV is calculated by the sum of all its assets minus the sum of its liabilities.)

But then the COVID-19 pandemic comes along in the spring of 2020. There is immediate uncertainty and people are scared. They start liquidating their shares of the mutual fund, the net asset value of which is falling in step with the price decline of its assets._

But one investor doesn't sell. She actually buys more shares of the fund, doing so while prices are lower in the belief that they will eventually rise again.

The market keeps going down. Nozama stock also goes down, and the "herd" is now starting to panic. Redemptions start happening faster.

The fund manager now has to make a choice. The last thing he wants to do is sell the fund's investments at a lower price. Remember, he still has a cash account, and he would rather use that cash to buy more stock when the price gets lower. Instead, he has to pay the emotionally charged herd that is demanding their money back.

At a certain point after so many redemptions have been paid, the fund manager will have to start selling off investments to replenish the cash fund.

The manager originally bought Nozama stock for $2,000 a share. Its price during better days was as high as $3,000, but amid the pandemic it has fallen to $2,500. Because of redemption demands and the depletion of his cash fund, the manager sells a large part of his Nozama block at $2,500, still realizing a 25 percent gain.

Now comes the surprising part for many people.

Sometime in late January of the following year, people who were in the fund in 2020 get an IRS form 1099 saying they have taxable income on gains realized by the fund during the previous year. They are stunned and ask, "How can this be?" Their fund shares were down some 20 to 30 percent when they sold out—at the worst possible time, as it turned out—when the fund price was at its lowest. And they still have to pay a capital gains tax?

Even the investor who held the line has questions. The price of his fund shares has rebounded, thank goodness, but he never sold anything. He wonders how he incurred a capital gain without selling anything at a profit? Besides, Nozama stock was $2,900 a share when he first bought into the fund. The manager sold large blocks of it at $2,500. How, he asks, is that a gain on my part?

The answer for all of these folks lies in the "herd nature" of a mutual fund.

As noted earlier, the fund consists of many individuals invested in the same pool of stocks, meaning each individual is tied to "herd money." When the fund manager sells a stock and realizes a gain, the tax on that gain is shared by all individuals swimming in that pool. That is why fund investors receive a 1099 saying they had a taxable gain from a fund whose shares they sold for a loss.

(Keep in mind that if a mutual fund is owned in a retirement account such as an IRA or Roth, capital gains [or losses] are not recognized. This is why mutual funds are often best held in IRA or Roth accounts and not in a taxable brokerage account. How you own different investments and the types of accounts they are in can reduce unnecessary taxation.)

The problem for the investor who held onto his fund shares amid the rush of selling by others is slightly different, but tied to the same concept. The price of Nozama stock went down during his time in the fund (from $2,900 a share when he bought into the fund to $2,500 when the manager sold it). But our investor still has to pay tax on the full 25 percent gain the manager realized after buying Nozama at $2,000 and selling at $2,500. The investor, in effect, must pay tax on the gains realized by others on what for him is a depreciating asset. This is what I call a "loser's tax."

When Your Gain Becomes My Gain

Let's take a quick look here at capital gains and how they are taxed.

Under the current tax laws, if you purchase an investment and it gains value, you don't pay taxes until you sell. That's when you realize your gain (or loss) on the investment. It could be valued five times higher than what you paid for it, but if you're holding and not selling, then you don't pay taxes. It works the same way with real estate. If you buy an empty lot and hold it for 20 years, you don't pay taxes on it until you sell it. You'll pay *property* taxes every year based on the land value, but you don't pay capital gains tax on any growth in value until you sell it.

With a mutual fund, that's not the way it works. You pay taxes on any gains realized from the sale of assets within the fund. Let's also note here that most fund managers are actively buying and selling assets, meaning they are likely to incur taxable gains each year that will be shared with all investors in the fund.

One final comment on capital gains. Don't overlook the tax-strategic value of *capital losses* that result from selling an asset for less than you paid for it. Capital losses can be deducted from capital gains (up to a capped amount each year) and can be used strategically to limit taxes.

We'll look more closely at how capital gains are taxed—*SPOILER ALERT: they are taxed at a lower rate than ordinary income*—in the next chapter.

Bottom line: Mutual funds encouraged more people to invest in stocks, which was a good thing. The downside, however, is that each individual investor is at the mercy of the herd. And if the herd panics and begins a stampede to safety, even those who try to stay above the fray can get crushed in a tax crunch.

| Tax Secret #8 | Don't invest in ways that you lose control of when you pay your taxes. |

That's why it's important to invest your taxable brokerage accounts in financial vehicles that give you more control of when taxes are generated on the investments, not leaving it up to herd mentality and a mutual fund manager's discretion.

CHAPTER 7

How to Tame Your Tax Dragon

We've touched previously on the importance—especially in retirement—of having money in tax-free accounts as opposed to tax-deferred ones. The logic is pretty simple: if you can take more income on a tax-free basis, you'll pay less in taxes and keep more of your hard-earned retirement savings in your pocket.

We've also talked about the taxes incurred when moving money out of tax-deferred accounts—whether you *want* to or *have* to do so—as well as the strategic value of paying those taxes at a time (such as today) when tax rates are reduced. Again, the reasoning is pretty basic: if you've got to pay taxes on your tax-deferred retirement accounts eventually—and you will—why not do so at a reduced rate?

We'll spend much of this chapter looking more deeply at the difference between tax-deferred and tax-free retirement accounts. Specifically, between "defined-contributions" programs such as the 401(k) as well as the "traditional" IRA, and their counterpart on the opposite end of the tax spectrum, the tax-free Roth IRA. We'll also explore ways of strategically moving money from one to the other.

Individual Retirement Accounts

IRA Type	Contribution Limit	Catch-up at 50+	Income Limits
Traditional nondeductible	6,000	1,000	None
Traditional deductible	6,000	1,000	If covered by a plan; 109,000 - 129,000 joint 68,000 - 78,000 Single, HOH 0 - 10,000 married filing separately If one spouse is covered by a plan: 204,000 - 214,000 joint.
Roth	6,000	1,000	204,000 - 214,000 Joint 129,000 - 144,000 Single & HOH 0 - 10,000 married filing separately
Roth conversion			No income limit

But we first need a quick refresher course on tax brackets, an understanding of which is necessary when considering whether (or when) to move money out of tax-deferred accounts, an event that comes with an immediate tax obligation.

It is possible, you see, to pay your retirement taxes too fast. For example: If you have a $500,000 IRA and you move that money all at once into a tax-free Roth, you'll pay taxes through the nose on the entire half-million-dollar conversion. The better strategy is to transfer money incrementally in years when your taxable income is low enough that you can make transfers without being elevated into a higher tax bracket. A Roth IRA conversion can cause some major tax issues if you have another taxable event showing up unexpectedly in the same year. You have to do some serious tax planning to navigate that, and this requires a basic understanding of how tax brackets function.

A Tax Bracket Primer

In the U.S., there's what we call the marginal tax rate. It's based on your income, and as your income increases, so does your tax rate. It's called "progressive taxation."

Determining your tax bracket each year begins with establishing your adjusted gross income (AGI). This is your annual gross income—all wages, dividends, capital gains, business income, retirement distributions, and other ordinary income—minus certain "adjustments to income" such as retirement plan contributions, alimony payments, and student loan interest among others.

Once you've determined your AGI you then subtract deductions, either by itemizing them or taking the standard deduction. For a married couple filing jointly in 2022, the standard deduction was $25,900. The end result is your taxable income, the figure that determines where you sit within a tax bracket.

2022 IRS Tax Brackets

SINGLE FILER		MARRIED FILING JOINTLY	
Taxable Income	**Tax Bracket**	**Taxable Income**	**Tax Bracket**
$0-$10,275	10%	$0-$20,550	10%
$10,276-$41,775	12%	$20,551-$83,550	12%
$41,776-$89,075	22%	$83,551-$178,150	22%
$89,076-$170,050	24%	$178,151-$340,100	24%
$170,051-$215,950	32%	$340,101-$431,900	32%
$215,951-$539,900	35%	$431,901-$647,850	35%
$539,901 and above	37%	$647,851 and above	37%

Source: "IRS provides tax inflation adjustments for tax year 2022." www.irs.gov

2022 Standard Deduction

Single Filer	$12,950
Married Filing Jointly	$25,900
Head of Household	$19,400

A misconception many people have about tax brackets needs to be dispelled before we go further. Many people believe that if your taxable income puts you into, say, the 22 percent tax bracket, you will owe the IRS 22 percent on all taxable income. Fortunately, that's not how it works.

Under the tax brackets in place in 2022, a married couple with an AGI of, say, $110,000 would have taxable income of around $85,000 after taking the $25,900 standard deduction. Their income would be taxed at 10 percent on the first $20,550, 12 percent on the next amount up to $83,550, and 22 percent on any amount beyond that. That is how progressive taxation works.

Make Full Use of the Roth IRA

The couple described above is in position to employ some strategies that could reduce their tax bracket, and consequently their taxes, in the future.

They are, for example, a prime candidate for a Roth conversion(s) that would help them take more future income from a tax-free source. In doing so, they will also experience some other advantages of the Roth that include:

- Future tax-free growth
- No annual Required Minimum Distribution
- The ability to pass a Roth to beneficiaries on a tax-free basis

With taxable income of $84,000 in 2022, this couple was in the lower end of the 22 percent bracket. They could, if they wanted, take on additional taxable income in one or more years—which they would do when making a Roth conversion—before being elevated into the 24 percent bracket that in 2022 began with taxable income of more than $178,150 (for a married couple filing jointly). Granted, the size of any conversion they might make will depend on the size of tax bite they are willing to take in any year of a transfer. But the point remains that they are in a good position to make this decision without moving into a higher bracket.

By making a Roth conversion in years before tax rates rise, our couple might be able to enter a lower tax bracket even as they maintain their gross income at current or even slightly higher levels. By taking more income from a tax-free source such as the Roth IRA, their taxable income could fall below the $83,550 threshold that in 2022 separates the 12 and 22 percent tax bracket.

Our couple might also be able to reduce their tax rate through strategic use of capital gains and "qualified" dividends, a strategy made possible by controlling your taxable income.

As noted in the previous chapter, capital gains taxes are paid on the growth of an asset—stocks, bonds, real estate, precious metals, a business—but they can be something of a friend in tax planning. This is because capital gains are taxed at a considerably lower rate than is ordinary income. In fact, some taxpayers—people with between $0 and $83,350 in taxable income (as of 2022)—pay *no tax* on capital gains. People with between $83,351 and $517,200 in taxable income pay a 15 percent tax, while higher earners pay a 20 percent capital gains tax.

Higher earners, however, can also face an additional tax on investment income. The Net Investment Income Tax (NIIT) is an additional 3.8 percent tax imposed on net investment earnings (all realized gains minus investment expenses) for persons with modified adjusted gross income exceeding $200,000 for a single filer or $250,000 for a couple filing jointly. Realized gains include capital gains, dividends, interest, rental property income, and any other income derived from investment.

In essence, most people facing a 20 percent tax on capital gains are in reality paying a 23.8 percent tax because of the NIIT. I call this another of the "hidden taxes" of the IRS tax code, one that adds insult to injury for people who earn and invest well.

The same income thresholds that apply to capital gains taxes also apply to taxes on "qualified dividends," which also are taxed at a lower rate—the same as capital gains—than are ordinary dividends.

Determining whether a dividend is qualified or ordinary can be complex. But as a rule of thumb, most dividends from American corporations are considered qualified if their stock is held for at least 60 days during a 121-day period that begins 60 days prior to the declaration of a dividend.[16] It's enough for most people to know that a broker or investment firm will sort out qualified and ordinary dividends on IRS Form 1099, and that seeking out ways of realizing qualified dividends is a tax-saving strategy you should discuss with your advisor.

These are some of the strategies we employ in our TaxSmart planning process at Secured Retirement.

Tax talk, as we know well, can be confusing for many people. Throwing around all these numbers can make your eyes water. That's why I suggest that unless you're comfortable with tax returns and investment taxation rules, you may be best served getting professional advice. For as a mentor of mine told me early in my career, "Don't ever cut your own hair if paying a professional can keep you from embarrassment."

A do-it-yourself approach to tax planning, if done without proper knowledge of how taxes work, can be quite expensive. It's like saving a few bucks and getting a bad haircut. Let a professional, such as a member of my team, help you lower your tax burden by exploring ways to lower your taxable income and marginal tax rate through strategies dealing with income, investments, distributions, and deductions.

---

[16]"Questions and Answers on the Net Investment Income Tax." Nov. 23, 2021. www.irs.gov

Contributions vs. Conversions: Same Sound, Different Song

Blessed with the benefit of hindsight, we can easily say that the couple described above would have been well-advised to build up a bucket of tax-free money by making Roth IRA *contributions* earlier in life.

But that's the wonderful thing about hindsight; it's always 20/20. It's easy to say a younger worker should have been making *after-tax contributions* to a Roth, then never again have to pay tax on that growing pool of money. But reality tells us a different story. Putting *pretax* money into a 401(k), 403(b) or IRA provided an immediate tax break that kept more money in our pocket when we needed every penny to raise families, pay for college, buy a home, or start a new business.

Still, it's never too late to make strategic Roth *conversions* at an opportune time—specifically, when you can do so without affecting your tax bracket, and when tax rates are lower.

Please take note of the difference between "contributions" to a retirement plan and "conversions" into a Roth. I've found that because "conversion" and "contribution" sound similar, many people confuse the rules around these tax moves. But there is a big difference between the two, and you need to understand that difference.

Contributions

A "contribution" involves putting money into a traditional IRA, a Roth IRA, or a "defined-contribution" plan such as an employer-offered 401(k) or 403(b). These contributions may be made on either a pretax basis for a traditional IRA or 401(k), or an after-tax basis for a Roth.

These annual contributions are limited. In 2022, an individual under age 50 could make a $6,000 annual contribution to an IRA (this applies to either a traditional or Roth IRA, but the total contribution to both cannot exceed $6,000). People aged 50 and older were allowed an additional $1,000 "catch-up" contribution.

The contribution limit for a 401(k) is considerably higher. In 2022, workers under age 50 could defer up to $20,500, with that limit rising to $27,000 for workers 50 and older. There also is a "combined" contribution limit—money invested by both an employee and an employer—of $61,000 in 2022. Employees aged 50 and older have the opportunity to defer up to $67,500 from all sources.

Most contributions to a traditional IRA are tax-deductible for the year in which they are made, but not all are.

The tax-deductible status of contributions is subject to an earnings test as well as to whether an individual or at least one member of a married couple was covered by an employer retirement plan. People not covered at work can generally deduct all of their IRA contributions (up to the contribution limit) from the income they report to the IRS. People who are covered by a workplace retirement plan will find the deductions on their contributions subject to limitations determined by their modified adjusted gross income (MAGI). The chart below shows the differences.

2022 IRA Deduction Limits

For employees not covered by a retirement plan at work

Filing Status	MAGI	Allowed Deduction
Single/head of Household	Any amount	Full deduction up to contribution limit
Married filing jointly *Neither spouse covered at work*	Any amount	Full deduction up to contribution limit
Married filing jointly *With one spouse covered at work*	$204,000 or less	Full deduction up to contribution limit
	$204,000 to $214,000	Partial deduction
	$214,000 or more	No deduction

Employees covered by a retirement plan at work

Filing Status	MAGI	Allowed Deduction
Single/head of Household	$68,000 or less	Full deduction up to contribution limit
Single/head of Household	$68,001 to $78,000	Partial deduction
Single/head of Household	$78,000 or more	No deduction
Married filing jointly	$109,000 or less	Full deduction up to contribution limit
Married filing jointly	$109,000 to $129,000	Partial deduction
Married filing jointly	$129,000 or more	No deduction

Source: www.irs.gov

Moreover, not everyone can make a "direct" contribution to a Roth IRA.

In 2022, a married couple filing jointly with MAGI exceeding $210,000 ***could not*** contribute directly to a Roth. Couples with MAGI under $204,000 could contribute up to the allowed limit, and couples with MAGI between $204,000 and $214,000 could make a partial contribution.

Let's also note here that Roth *contributions* require earned income—wages, tips, business or self-employment income—for eligibility. If you're not currently receiving employment compensation, you cannot make a Roth contribution for the year in question.

But even high earners can make a *nondeductible* contribution to a traditional IRA. Nondeductible IRA contributions do not generate a reduction in taxable income for the year they are made, but the contribution is not taxed when withdrawals are made. (This assumes your tax preparer completes the proper IRS tax form and the contributions remain tracked.)

Conversions Are Treated Differently

A conversion is the act of moving money from a tax-deferred account into a tax-free Roth. The amount of money converted is typically a taxable event, unless the original contribution had already been taxed as is the case with a nondeductible contribution. (More on this last part is upcoming in our discussion of the "backdoor Roth conversion.")

An important distinction to make about conversions is that they are *not subject* to the income limits on contributions. (Such limits once existed, but were removed in 2010.) Today, everyone who has an existing IRA or 401(k) can move money to a Roth account. Furthermore, the amount that can be moved is unlimited. You also do not need earned income to do a conversion.

One other important distinction to make between contributions and conversions. A contribution can be made up to the filing date (usually April 15) of the tax year in question. In other words, you could reduce your 2021 taxable income by making an IRA contribution as late as April of 2022.

Conversions, on the other hand, must be completed by December 31 of the tax year being reported. This creates both a challenge and a possible pitfall. If you knew on January 1 every year what your taxable income was going to be, you could more easily manage a Roth IRA conversion and end up at year-end in the tax bracket you are trying to maintain. If you're on a fixed income or have predictable wages, that may be possible. For many business owners, however, that's not so easy, especially if you have a year like 2020 when a black swan event disrupts the economy and makes your income more difficult to predict.

The Backdoor Roth: The IRS's Best Kept Tax Secret

A lot of times, someone will come into our office and say they can't contribute to a Roth IRA because they earn too much income, as detailed above. That may well be the case for a Roth *contribution*, but it is not the case for a *conversion*. This is the basis for what has come to be known as the "backdoor Roth."

Since there is no limit to how much money you can move from a traditional IRA or 401(k) into a Roth, you can contribute the maximum amount allowable to either and then convert to a Roth IRA at any time. You'll still pay taxes on the money you move, but you can use that strategy to set up future tax-free withdrawals that will lower your taxable income and help manage your marginal tax rate.

The backdoor Roth IRA conversion, in short, is an opportunity for high-income earners to take full advantage of the Roth's tax mitigation possibilities. Backdoor Roth IRAs are tricky, however, and I recommend working with a tax professional before attempting to do one.

Let's say you're a married couple earning $300,000 a year. You earn too much to make a traditional IRA or Roth contribution. But you can make a nondeductible contribution to your retirement account and then convert it into a Roth IRA. That way, you're following the rules but also taking advantage of a tax-mitigation strategy that the rules allow. You can get your money into a Roth IRA without contributing to it directly. You will have entered the world of future tax-free income through the back door.

The key to doing this conversion, as is the case with all Roth conversions, is not elevating yourself into a higher tax bracket.

Let's consider the married couple above with $300,000 in taxable income. In 2022, they were in the 24 percent tax bracket. They could take on an additional $40,000 in taxable income before making the rather significant jump into the 32 percent bracket, a 33 percent increase over their current level.

Our couple might, however, be able to make more than a $40,000 Roth conversion without jumping into the next tax bracket. This is because the IRS does not group all money in an IRA together for taxation purposes. Our couple, remember, made both deductible (tax-deferred) and nondeductible (already taxed) contributions to their IRA. When moving that money into a Roth, the IRS uses a pro rata rule to determine what part of the conversion is tax-deferred money and must be taxed.

Let's say our couple has a $100,000 IRA of which $93,000 was made (and grown) through deductible contributions and $7,000 through nondeductible contributions. They want to do a Roth conversion, but they worry that any amount above $40,000 will bump them into the 32 percent tax bracket that in 2022 began at $340,100. But they might, with the careful guidance of a tax professional, convert slightly more than $40,000 upon learning that 7 percent of the conversion can be moved tax-free.

When done with proper planning, the Roth IRA conversion can be used as a strategy to help you manage your taxes by lowering your taxable income. But again, the key to doing this effectively is avoiding big jumps from one tax bracket to another. That's where having a basic understanding of how tax brackets are structured is necessary.

Optimize Your Marginal Tax Rate

Tax Secret #9	Optimize your tax brackets. Take advantage of low-income years to increase taxable income but control income so you don't inadvertently jump into a higher bracket.

We often see families that are not managing their tax brackets very well. For instance, when their taxable income is low, they're not taking advantage of the opportunity to avoid future taxes by moving money from their traditional IRA or 401(k) to a Roth IRA. Consequently, when they later take money from a tax-deferred account—either because they need it for income or want to move it to a tax-free source—they may find that tax rates are higher and their withdrawal will cost them more in taxes than in previous years.

Another way families don't manage their tax brackets well is by taking too much out of their traditional IRA at one time. They may be trying to do the right thing but find they've increased their taxable income to the point that they moved into a higher tax bracket.

I don't mean to be overly critical here. I know how unexpected things often happen in life, No one can predict the future, and the best-laid plans can go asunder. I've known people, for instance, who early in a year began moving money from their tax-deferred accounts into a Roth. It seemed like a good idea at the time, and it was. They were in a position to take on some additional taxable income without bumping themselves into a higher bracket, so they did it. Good for them.

But then, well, stuff happens. Good stuff, we hope. People may suddenly realize an unexpected financial windfall. An inheritance, perhaps, or maybe an unanticipated bump in business profits, a well-deserved raise, or a better-paying job. Suddenly they find themselves in a higher tax bracket, and the purchasing power of their windfall is less than expected because of higher taxes.

And then we have the flipside of the coin.

Just as there are times when your income can skyrocket, there are also times when your income can drop precipitously. If you own your own business, for instance, you could earn $500,000 in one year, then the next year you might only earn $135,000. That huge drop from one year to the next could see you move from the 35 percent tax bracket to the 24 percent tax bracket. Similar declines in annual income could result from a long-term layoff or loss of a job. A major market decline also could adversely affect income.

Such economic declines are a bad break, no doubt. But they also present an opportunity.

A decline in annual income and subsequent drop in marginal tax rate may provide a timely opportunity to move money out of your tax-deferred accounts. Here is a case where you might actually need this money to replace lost income, but there's also a chance to put some away for the future in a tax-free account. As the old adage says: When one door closes, another opens.

Don't overlook, either, the tax deductions available through charitable donations, which we'll discuss in more depth in the next chapter.

Let's also note here that an elevation into a higher tax bracket isn't always a budget breaker, especially if it's a short-term visit.

A person taking on additional taxable income that elevates them from the high end of the 10 percent bracket to the low end of the 12 percent one—the bracket in which most Americans find themselves—likely won't feel a painful tax bite. The same might be said for someone making the small step up from the 22 to the 24 percent bracket. Keep in mind, too, that people in, say, the 22 percent bracket don't pay that rate on all their taxable income, but only the part that exceeds $83,550—the threshold between the 12 and 22 percent brackets in 2022.

Other jumps, however, are more costly. An elevation from the 12 percent bracket to the 22 is significant, an 83 percent increase. Going from the 22 to the 24 percent bracket seems tolerable, but the leap from 24 to 32 is a nasty 33 percent bump.

The challenge is to try to smooth out the bumps and remain in the lowest tax bracket you can realize.

You've likely heard tax experts talk about the ideal tax bracket: 0 percent. That seems like an unattainable dream to many taxpayers, but it's possible for people living on taxable income that falls below the standard deduction ($25,900 for couples in 2022). And one needn't live like a hermit to pay no federal or state taxes. A couple living off distributions from tax-free sources, who receive their Social Security benefits tax-free, who have long-term capital gains or qualified dividends, and possibly use the tax-free "living benefits" of some whole life insurance policies, might well find themselves paying little or even nothing in taxes.

Digging Deeper

Let's make a brief diversion here and look at the tax differences between money in a brokerage account and that in a traditional IRA.

Let's assume you have $1 million in a brokerage account—congratulations—that pays a 3 percent annual dividend, or $3,000 in taxable income. Now let's say you withdraw $100,000 from this account. How will you be taxed? You will be taxed only on the growth and dividend portion of that amount as the principal has already been taxed. Moreover, any capital gains and qualified dividends are taxed at either 15 or 20 percent (or at 23.8 percent, if the 3.8 percent Net Investment Income Tax applies), far below the rate on ordinary income. But if you withdraw $100,000 from a traditional IRA, 100 percent of that will be taxed as ordinary income at your regular tax rate.

A more realistic challenge for most people is to limit taxes using strategies such as those we employ through our TaxSmart program. Paying less in taxes each year can add up to tens or hundreds of thousands of dollars over the course of a 20- to 30-year retirement.

Remember, every dollar you keep in your pocket instead of Uncle Sam's is an additional dollar for you to spend.

To repeat a point made frequently throughout this chapter and book, the best way to manage your taxes is to manage your tax rate. And the best way to do that is to drain your pool of tax-deferred retirement accounts, money that will be taxed eventually, and move those assets into tax-free accounts from which future withdrawals incur no taxes. Yes, draining the pool also means paying taxes on the water—money—removed, but there is an ideal time for doing that.

That time is right now.

Keep in mind that the Tax Cuts and Jobs Act of 2017 opened a window of lower tax rates, the lowest rates seen in four decades. But that window won't stay open forever. As noted previously, this legislation has an expiration date. Unless Congress acts to extend its "sunset" provision, taxes are scheduled to go back to 2017 levels on January 1, 2016. But as this book was being completed in early 2022, we still are looking at a four-year window of opportunity, though politicians could close that window at any time.

Look, we don't know where tax rates are going to be in the future. We do know where they are now, and where they are scheduled to be through 2025. That's why it's important to maximize your opportunities now when tax brackets and rates are lower. This is why I encourage you to meet soon with me or one of my TaxSmart planners to begin the process of taming your tax beast while it's still possible.

CHAPTER 8

Charitable Gifting

C haritable gifting can be used to reduce taxable income, or even mitigate the taxes you incur when converting your traditional IRA into a tax-free Roth IRA.

One of the biggest mistakes families make regarding charitable gifting is not fully understanding the tax code regarding donations. Many consequently miss out on the tax advantages of gifting. They give freely to a Boy Scouts fundraiser outside the convenience store, to the Girl Scouts selling cookies door-to-door, to their church when it needs a little extra money, and to the bell ringers in front of the grocery store in their Santa suits. People usually give to their favorite causes through out-of-pocket cash or by writing checks.

Tax Secret #10	Optimize your charitable gifting by creating a customized strategy based on your age, planning, and investments.

While it's always an admirable thing to give in this way, there are also situations where families could take better advantage of the tax code by donating to the charity of their choice and giving themselves a tax break at the same time.

It's important to note before going further that the tax treatment of charitable gifts has changed somewhat in recent years. The Tax

Cuts and Jobs Act of 2017, while lowering tax brackets and doubling the standard deduction, also deemed that charitable contributions can be considered for tax purposes only when included among itemized deductions.[17] For all practical purposes, this means itemized deductions must exceed the amount of the standard deduction ($25,900 for couples filing jointly in 2022) in order for charitable contributions to be deducted from taxable income.

(We'll discuss ways to deal with this situation in the "Calendar Grouping" section later in this chapter.)

If, however, you are able to use itemized deductions instead of the standard deduction, some timely gifting may decrease your total tax bill. Let's look at some ways to do that.

Donate Noncash Assets to Charity

Donating noncash assets—stocks, bonds, mutual funds, real estate, precious metals, artwork, and so on—that have appreciated in value can provide not only a tax deduction (for the fair market value of the donated asset) but also a break from capital gains taxes.

The charity, in effect, pays your taxes for you after it sells your donated asset and converts it into cash. Most charities don't mind doing this because those with a 503(c)3 designation are not required to pay capital gains taxes. The donor gets a tax deduction for the entire value of the contribution, the charity gets the full value of the asset, and nobody pays capital gains taxes. This can be a sweet deal for everyone but the IRS, and you won't find me shedding tears for that group.

But not everyone is eager to donate an asset that has grown in value over time. Some people willing to donate an asset might prefer

[17]The CARES Act of 2019 allowed a $300 "top line" (non-itemized) deduction for single filer taxpayers, and a $600 deduction for couples filing jointly who made charitable cash contributions for the 2020 and 2021 tax years. Source: "Expanded tax benefits help individuals and businesses give to charity during 2021; deductions up to $600 available for cash donations by non-itemizers." Sept. 17, 2021. www.irs.gov

to sell on their own and then consider their options. They might give all proceeds from the sale to charity, or they might keep some of the proceeds—if they need the income, for example—and donate the remainder. Either way, the seller/donor in this case may incur a capital gains tax that could have been avoided by donating the appreciated asset in its entirety.

Having said that, let's keep several things in mind when talking about capital gains taxes:

One, long-term capital gains—profits from assets held for more than a year—are taxed at a considerably lower rate than ordinary income. Some people, in fact, pay *no tax* on long-term capital gains. In 2022, single filers with taxable income below $41,675, and couples filing jointly with taxable income below $83,350, paid no tax on long-term capital gains. Higher earners paid rates of either 15 or 20 percent, depending on their taxable income.

Two, the tax deduction you receive for your gift can offset some or all of your capital gains tax. Perhaps you've sold an asset for a profit and kept some of the proceeds. A charitable donation of any remaining proceeds can reduce or even negate capital gains taxes that can be troublesome, especially those on short-term gains (from the sale of assets held for less than a year) that are taxed as ordinary income.

Three, higher earners also need to be aware of an additional tax on net investment income (NII). People with modified adjusted gross incomes (MAGI) of $250,000 for a married couple filing jointly, and $200,000 for a single filer, could incur an additional tax of 3.8 percent on all investment gains—interest, dividends, capital gains, rental and royalty income among other sources—offset by investment losses and other investment expenses. The NII tax is one that active investors need to keep an eye on.

Fourth, don't overlook the value of a well-timed *capital loss*. Any asset sale that involves a loss can be used (up to an annual limit) to offset capital gains.

A Case Study in Giving

A friend of mine, Bob, worked for a big company for several years. During his tenure, he participated in the company's employee purchase plan and accumulated a large amount of company stock. One day, he decided to give $100,000 to his favorite charity, the American Red Cross. (Yes, Bob is generous, but the following example is also applicable to many of us who gift lower amounts.)

Had he sold his company stock to generate the $100,000 donation, Bob would have paid $15,000 in capital gains taxes and gifted $85,000 to the Red Cross. Bob instead decided to gift the organization the full stock amount, unsold. He consequently was able to deduct a $100,000 charitable contribution—the fair market value of his shares at the time of his donation—from his taxes, and the Red Cross got the full $100,000 charitable gift. It sold the stock to produce cash, but as a tax-exempt organization, it paid no capital gains taxes. That's what we call a win-win. Again, the only loser is the IRS, which lost the tax proceeds from the stock sale, albeit for a good cause.

But sometimes people get emotional about selling their stock. They own, say, Apple stock they've held for years, and it's appreciated considerably in value. They've attached some sentimental value to it. After all, it's been a winner for them, and they are very reluctant to give it up. They're not concerned about the capital gains taxes if they sell it, but they are looking for a tax deduction to offset, for example, additional taxable income from an RMD or an inherited IRA. So, they decide to sell their Apple stock and donate the proceeds in order to get the charitable tax deduction. But they also really, really, really want to stay involved with Apple.

They decide to sell with the idea that they can buy more Apple soon after. They can do this because they sold Apple at a profit. Had they sold Apple at a loss—and realized a capital loss they could write off against any capital gains—they could not have purchased more

Apple for 30 days because of something called the "wash-sale rule." This rule says you have to wait 30 days to buy a stock again after you sell it for a loss. If you do buy the stock again before the 30 days runs out, you can't take the capital loss deduction. The rule *does not* apply, however, after selling stock at a gain.

Over time, some people thought of a way to get around the "wash-sale" rule regarding the sale of depreciated assets. They bought additional shares of the devalued stock *before* selling what they already owned. The idea was to take a capital loss at the same time they were buying new shares that they hoped would appreciate in value over time. Clever, right?

It was so clever that the IRS stepped in to stop the practice. It expanded its wash-sale rules to include a 30-day period *prior* to a sale. As the tax code now stands, if you sell a stock for a loss, you can't buy it back within a 30-day window of selling it, before or after, or you forfeit your capital loss deduction. It's as if you never sold the stock at all.

People hear about that rule and think there's a 60-day waiting period on sales involving gains as well as losses. Some even think they can never buy the stock again after they sell it, which isn't the case.

If you sell a stock at a loss, you have to wait 30 days before you can buy that stock again. Additionally, you can't buy additional shares of a stock 30 days prior to selling it for a loss. But if you sell at a gain, the only downside is you have to wait a year to get the tax-favorable long-term capital gains treatment back on any future sales of that stock.

Back to my friend Bob and his highly appreciated Apple stock. He gives it away to charity, then rebuys Apple with cash in his savings account. He does not have to wait 30 days to do this because he gifted the stock at a gain. He can buy new shares of Apple immediately with the hope of realizing future gains. If he holds his new shares for longer than 365 days, he can sell them and incur only long-term capital gains that are taxed at either 15 or 20 percent. Bob doesn't plan to sell at any time less than a year to avoid short-term capital gains that are taxed as regular income.

Granted, the cost basis of Bob's newly purchased Apple shares will likely be higher than those he acquired over the years through his company's employee purchase plan. But Bob can live with this.

He was intending to make a $100,000 contribution to the Red Cross anyway. He did so by gifting a highly appreciated stock for which he received a tax deduction for the full amount. He gifted his shares at a price he might have sold at anyway. Moreover, his donation effectively scrubbed away his potential capital gains tax. Remember, the Red Cross sold the "Bob" shares it now owns, and the Red Cross pays no capital gains taxes as a tax-exempt organization.

Bob's strategy has other positive aspects. Because he gifted an appreciated asset, he could immediately purchase new shares of Apple, a stock he really likes and believes will continue to grow in value over time. In addition, the higher cost basis of the new purchase could mean lower capital gains on future sales. The higher cost basis also will be greatly appreciated by Bob's loved ones who might someday inherit his Apple holdings. This is because the cost basis of inherited stock is its trading price on the day of the donor's death. Bob's beneficiaries will inherit stock at a higher—and more tax-friendly—cost basis than if they inherited the shares Bob purchased at lower prices through the company plan.

Congress is considering eliminating the step-up basis in cases where stock passes to heirs. If that step-up cost basis rule goes away, you could benefit your heirs, as well as your charity and yourself, by using the stock donation strategy that includes eligibility for a quick repurchase, albeit at a likely higher cost, on a stock that's been a winner for you.

Calendar Grouping

As noted earlier, under the tax code in place since 2018, charitable contributions can be deducted only when included among itemized deductions. As a matter of practical sense, itemized deductions are used only when they exceed the standard deduction. Many Americans find using the standard deduction gives them a lower tax bill and thus are unable to deduct large charitable contributions.

One way around this is to gift a charitable organization twice in the same year through something we call "calendar grouping."

In 2022, for example, the standard deduction was $25,900 if you're married and filing jointly. Let's say your goal is to give $10,000 to your church every year. In December of 2022, you start looking ahead to the tax return you must file by the following April. (Good for you, by the way, for planning ahead.) You estimate that you will have $14,000 in other itemized deductions, and your charitable gift will put you at $24,000. At this point it's still to your advantage to take the higher standard deduction, meaning you will receive no tax break for the church contribution.

Here is a situation where you might consider giving your planned 2023 contribution a year early. Perhaps you donate an additional $10,000 in December 2022. Your itemized deductions now exceed the standard and you can claim a deduction for your $20,000 total contribution. If you choose not to make a contribution in 2023—figuring that you doubled your church donation in '22—you would likely take the standard deduction for that year.

Calendar grouping need not always be the "double or nothing" strategy described above. Some years you might consider "paying forward" your next year's planned contribution just enough to get you over the itemization threshold. Or, you might adjust your contributions from year to year depending on how your itemized deductions vary. Maybe you may have higher deductions in a year of a major medical procedure or losses in business. You might consider adjusting your charitable contributions depending on how they help you meet the itemization threshold and make maximum use of the tax deduction.

Putting Charitable Gifts on Hold for Future Use

Another thing we hear often is, "I don't want my charity to have $10,000 right now." You might want to make a contribution now, but you'd like it to be used at a later time, perhaps when your church or charity has a major building or fundraising project.

It may be time to consider ways to place charitable gifts in a holding area, a vault of sorts. The donor-advised fund (DAF) provides that opportunity.

This strategy works much the same way as the family foundations that wealthy people have used for years to set aside money—and gain tax-favorable treatment—for special causes. These foundations have their own governing boards, they have to file special tax returns, and must show their expenditures and follow all kinds of rules and regulations. But unless your name is Rockefeller, Carnegie, or Bill Gates, a family foundation with all its additional administration and expenses may not work for you. They are designed for the massively affluent.

On the other hand, there is a way to use a foundation-like structure even if you're not super rich. A donor-advised fund is comprised of donations from one or more individuals. The fund itself is controlled by a management organization that receives, grows, and ultimately distributes the contributions based on guidance from the contributor(s).

The DAF, in short, is a relatively easy way to make one or a series of tax-deductible charitable contributions through one organization. Contributors to a DAF get one receipt from the management company each year that shows total donations for the year. (A much easier record-keeping system for donors at tax-reporting time, in my opinion.) The management company will attempt to grow the donated assets over time before making charitable distributions at the direction of one or more donors to the fund.

Let's consider an example of how such a fund might work.

Your goal, as stated above, is to make a $10,000 annual contribution to your church. You like the idea of getting an annual tax deduction, but you also know the church has a major building project scheduled for three years down the road, and you'd like to see your money used on that project. So, you make your annual contribution to a donor-advised fund. You get your annual tax deduction, but the church—or any other IRS-defined charitable organization—doesn't get the money until you tell the fund to gift a contribution. Over time you might decide to contribute money from the fund to other charities, and you can direct the fund to make these contributions as well. You have, in effect, established your own foundation, one with the potential to live on (under the direction of your beneficiaries) long after you are gone.

There are some rules about how fast you can write off those charitable gifts, so it's wise to talk to your tax advisor or accountant first to make sure you're within the proper thresholds.

Consider the Qualified Charitable Distribution

Qualified charitable distributions (QCDs) are a way of using gifting to reduce or even eliminate taxes owed on a traditional IRA.

Beginning at age 70½, all owners of traditional IRAs can make direct donations from their IRAs to IRS-approved charitable organizations and have the value of their gift (to an annual limit of $100,000) deducted from taxable income. A qualified charitable distribution also can be part of a Required Minimum Distribution. Equally significant, it is *not necessary* to itemize deductions in order to take the tax deduction available through the QCD.

That, in my view, checks three significant boxes in the gift-giving tax strategy.

A couple of notes are necessary to understand before attempting to use the tax-favorable aspects of the QCD.

First, the contribution must be made directly to the IRS-approved charity. Any distribution check made out to the IRA owner is considered a taxable distribution, even if the money is immediately turned over to a charity. For a QCD to be tax deductible, the distribution check must be made out to the charity.

Second, a QCD cannot currently be made from a 401(k) or other defined-contribution retirement account.

The word *currently* is important because the rules regarding QCDs have changed frequently over time. Before 2015, the IRS often waited until January before deciding if QCD rules would apply to the previous tax year. The rules became permanent, however, in 2015.

Moreover, the starting age for QCD eligibility did not change when the starting age for RMDs did. The SECURE Act of 2019 changed the RMD starting age to 72 for people who had not reached age 70 as of July 1, 2019. Allowing an early window for a way to reduce one's pool of tax-deferred money is something I applaud. Is it too much to hope that the same opportunity might soon be extended to the 401(k) and other tax-deferred retirement accounts?

Finally, consider how the QCD can be an even more effective tax-planning tool than gifting stock directly to a charity.

That's primarily because it is an "above the line" (non-itemized) deduction, meaning this is money you don't have to claim as income. It can immediately reduce adjusted gross income, a key starting point in determining things such as taxable income and the threshold for taxation of Social Security benefits. An above-the-line deduction is especially helpful for families that cannot otherwise deduct charitable contributions because they do not have enough itemized deductions.

My recommendation for anyone over 70½ years old with a traditional IRA is to consider the qualified charitable distribution, a gifting vehicle with more upside than even a donor-advised fund or a family foundation, and certainly more than writing checks directly out of your checkbook. Those charitable gifts may not be deducted.[18]

---

[18]"Limits on Deductions." Page 14, IRS Publication 525, "Charitable Contributions." March 2021

CHAPTER 9

Seek Professional Advice

Just as the people of Pompeii failed to heed the earth-shaking rumbles that forecast the fateful eruption of Mount Vesuvius, many Americans today fail to prepare for the tax firestorm looming on their horizon.

It doesn't have to be that way. Not when we have advance warning about the inevitable eruption of tax-deferred money—money that will be taxed eventually— building up just beneath the surface of our daily lives. Not when we have time to seek shelter from the storm, to take defensive measures *today* to move ourselves to a safer harbor, much as Pliny the Younger did in his timely evacuation of Pompeii.

And so, we'll talk one last time in this final chapter about dealing with the upcoming tax storm that awaits so many people in retirement. We'll recap ways of protecting ourselves from the impending raid on the retirement savings we accumulated over a lifetime of hard work and sacrifice. We'll talk about how most people in retirement find it more important to keep the wealth they have as opposed to increasing that wealth. We'll talk yet again about how reducing taxes is one of the best ways to keep more of what you have.

We'll talk about transitioning into a completely new phase of life, from our accumulation years in the daily workforce into the preservation/distribution phase of retirement. We'll talk about the changes in mindset—and sometimes in financial advisors—that are necessary when moving from building wealth to generating our own paychecks from that wealth. We'll talk about the importance of making that money last throughout retirement.

We'll talk, in short, about how a TaxSmart™ planning professional can help you avoid the potholes on the road between you and the retirement of your dreams.

Getting There Is Half the Fun, and Worth the Effort

I fervently hope that no one reading this book—or who hears my radio programs in the Twin Cities area or meets with my team in our office—ever forgets the hard work and sacrifice that goes into building what is commonly called a "retirement nest egg."

Your years of raising a family can be some of the toughest, and ultimately most rewarding, of your life. Money was tight, yet you somehow managed to put some of it into your retirement account. Good for you. That's money that could have gone to Disney, or to buy a new car, a house, or something special for your family. Instead, you invested whatever you could whenever you could in your own future. Kudos is in order.

Essentially, that money in your retirement account is a sacrifice. You sacrificed your current income for future retirement planning. This process, known as "wealth accumulation," likely began in your late 20s or 30s, then accelerated in your 40s and 50s.

The goal during our years in the workforce, in part, is to create as large a balance sheet as we can. We build up assets that will be available for future income in retirement when employment no longer provides a regular paycheck. The financial industry is aware of this objective, and most of its messaging over the years—to Boomers, Generation X, and now Millennials—focuses on one thing. Grow your wealth. Whatever you do, however you do it, grow your wealth. It's the message screamed at us from the covers of money magazines and financial services advertisements on network programming and business channels alike.

Over the course of those years, your wealth advisor, your investment advisor, or your broker were all focused on increasing your wealth. Nothing wrong with that. Their total focus was on returns and finding the right balance of risk versus reward. To that end, going back to the 1980s, the families that found the right risk/reward balance in their investment portfolios generally grew the most wealth.

But things change as your approach or enter your 50s and prepare for a new phase of life.

Times Change, and So Must We

Perhaps you noticed that most financial professionals focus primarily on asset growth and wealth accumulation. You've probably also noticed that much of this planning is centered around the products and tools that my industry uses to accomplish growth. Discussions and decisions typically involve what mutual funds to invest in. Do I have enough bonds in my portfolio? Do I need an annuity? Is life insurance needed, or what should I do with the term policy taken out 20 years ago now that the kids are out of the house and on their own?

At Secured Financial, we approach things a bit differently.

Sure, we offer much of this same investment advice and wealth management strategies to our clients. But we hear more often from families whose needs have changed over time. They no longer need the same advice they sought in their younger years when they first began setting aside and growing the money that would become the building blocks of a secure retirement. Now in their 50s or 60s, most people we see are seeking help with matters that arise as they approach what I call "the golden decade," a period of five years preceding and following retirement. Their financial mindset has shifted, as it should. Their new concerns are reflected in the comments we typically hear as we begin our TaxSmart™ Retirement Planning process. Among those we hear most often:

- Joe, we're at the stage in our life where our primary goal is to ensure that we have an income plan in place that will provide us with paychecks for the rest of our lives. We want to know that we can spend this money with the confidence that it will be there throughout our retirement years. There are things we'd like to do early in retirement while we're still able to do them, but we don't want to be forced to make drastic lifestyle changes later to keep our money from running out. We need to know we have a plan in place to cover health care or long-term care costs if we incur them.

- Can you share strategies on how to morally, ethically, and legally reduce the amount of taxes that we or our family will spend from this point forward? We are looking for proactive strategies that will save us money in the long term amid a rising tax environment.

- If you can help us grow our wealth, that would be great. Continued growth is still important to us, but not more important than taking back our money in a tax-efficient way while making sure it will last throughout our lifetime.

These are the issues people seem most interested in understanding. Consequently, the kind of planning I talk about is different from the wealth accumulation strategy most advisors deal with.

Most financial and investment advisors think they are being hired to manage investment strategies based on the modern portfolio theory. They focus on building a sound investment portfolio through diversification and investment optimization. They try to pick investments that are conservative, moderate, or aggressive based on the client's risk aversion profile. They concentrate on the structure of a portfolio while paying little attention to some of the biggest drains on these investments.

I'm talking about—you guessed it—taxes.

It's my belief that families that fail today to address the impact of taxes in the future will find themselves with less spending power in their retirement nest egg in 10, 20, or 30 years. Their savings will have less impact than those of people who worked to reduce future taxes *now* by paying some or all of them while tax rates are lower than we've seen in some 40 years.

I often have to remind clients that wealth accumulation is different from income or tax planning. Wealth accumulation is a higher-risk process of acquiring assets. The goal of income planning, however, is to ensure that these accumulated assets provide a family with retirement income they can spend in confidence while maintaining their lifestyle throughout retirement.

To be able to do that, however, requires preserving as much of your accumulated wealth as you can. Reducing what you owe in taxes is a key part of doing that.

Tax Secret #11	Get TaxSmart™ planning advice.

Seek Professional Help from a TaxSmart Advisor

The best way to ensure you do that is to hire a financial professional who takes a more comprehensive approach to retirement planning. By that I mean, start looking beyond investments and put an actual plan in your planning.

Keep in mind that investment advisors generally are not paid according to the amount of planning they do. They might earn a commission from the sale of a product, or collect a fee based on the assets they have under management. But when it comes to, say, advising you on the best time to begin taking Social Security benefits, they receive no extra compensation for that.

(It's possible, in fact, for an advisor to be biased if asked to provide Social Security guidance. You should ask yourself: Is my advisor suggesting I take benefits early because it's the best option for me, or is it because by taking income from the government, I won't be tapping the assets he manages and is compensated for accordingly?)

The same can be said of tax planning. An accountant might command a fee for dispensing tax advice, but tax planning is usually not on a financial advisor's fee schedule. Besides, many people wouldn't want to pay for the actual value that real tax planning can deliver.

At Secured Retirement, however, talking about tax-saving strategies is an essential part of our TaxSmart™ Planning. This is a customized and comprehensive level of financial service that includes investments and wealth management as well as tax planning, income planning, health-care and estate planning. Our professionals look at your individual or family financial situation and recommend a long-range income plan that includes tax-reducing strategies. We also include planning for possible future long-term care needs as well as providing for loved ones when you are no longer able to do so.

Our fee for this service is about the same as most investment advisors. We're not the cheapest and we're not the most expensive. Where we differ from some other firms is in offering detailed planning that covers the full range of our financial and physical needs in retirement as opposed to dealing only with investment strategies.

How you approach your retirement planning, including ways to keep more of your money in your pocket, is entirely up to you, of course. But please allow me to suggest that, as is the case with many things in life, you usually get what you pay for.

I've known people who attempt the do-it-yourself approach. They set up an account with Fidelity or Robinhood, then manage their own portfolio. These product providers do not offer additional services. They don't make stock recommendations or tell you if you have too many bonds in your portfolio. They won't tell you if you're too diversified, or not diversified enough. And they don't take responsibility if your investments tank. They just provide the platform and the tools for you to make your own decisions and leave you at your own mercy. And don't even think of asking about tax, income or estate planning strategies.

Other people will take an additional step and seek out investment strategists.

Most professionals in the financial planning industry fall into this category. They make investment recommendations, tell you if you're not diversified enough or if you're overweight in stocks versus bonds. They give you investment models that are mostly templated; you either fit their mold or you don't. If your investments go down, they will take responsibility for making bad picks, but you still lose money. And, you still have to pay them.

Again, the choice is up to you. My personal recommendation, given all the complexities of retirement and the role taxes can play during those years, is to find someone who does real planning as opposed to merely building a portfolio.

Look to the Future Today

While I've been known to hold a client's hand occasionally during trying times, I don't pretend to be a palm reader or a fortune teller. Nor am I a political scientist who reads the blowing of the Washington winds, yet I feel comfortable in making this one political prediction.

Our taxes are going up, probably sooner than later.

I'll leave the discussion of the reason for higher future taxes to others. The need to pay down national debt, a desire to increase social services, the rising costs of health care, the higher costs of maintaining a national defense—yeah, it's all part of it. I won't guess when higher tax rates are coming, but I can see them looming on the horizon.

Beyond that, we know this much for certain: If Congress does nothing before December 31, 2025, on January 1, 2026, taxes are scheduled to increase by reverting to their higher levels of pre-2018. However, I suspect we will see tax increases even before 2026.

Given the state of things right now, it's important to understand the hard reality that taxes today are lower than we've seen in the past 40 years, and probably at the lowest level we're going to see for the next several generations. This provides the perfect opportunity to add tax planning strategies to your retirement plan now. The opportunity to pay inevitable retirement taxes now when rates are lower is an option that is too good to pass up.

The years 2018 through 2025 will be a time, I fear, when many will look back and realize we could have done more to reduce our future taxes. As this book is being completed in early 2022, there is still a four-year window (barring congressional action) in which to make that happen. This is the opportunity of a lifetime and, sadly, most people are going to miss it.

Again, how you prepare for the impending tax storm is entirely up to you. Everyone's situation is different. You may be married or single. You may be supporting one child or five, or even two ex-spouses with multiple kids. You may have capital gains or capital losses. You may have received a promotion or a significant raise, or you may have been laid off. There is no boilerplate tax strategy that covers everyone.

But there is this. Most readers of this book are sitting on a pool of tax-deferred money from workplace plans or individual retirement accounts. All the people described above will pay tax on this money someday, or their inheritors will. All have the opportunity to pay those taxes now while rates are lower, giving them future tax-free growth and distributions in future years when taxes are likely to be higher than they are now.

Given all of the above, I encourage you to develop an income and tax plan that takes advantage of the low-rate climate in place today. Give me a call and I'll set you up with your own customized tax and income plan to help you reduce your taxes in retirement and set you up to maximize your tax brackets, now and in the future.

Made in the USA
Middletown, DE
27 May 2022

66273278R00076